Praise for the workshop that lead to the book...

...your business or your life

8 steps for getting all you want out of BOTH

"Combine Tom Peters and Tony Robbins and you start to understand David Shepherd's impact on the small business owner."

—Bill Branson
Phoenix, AZ

"The changes are mind-blowing, but it's going to be great!"

—Val Lenington, CMP
Ultimate Ventures, Inc.

"This material is about more than business mastery, it's about life mastery!"

—Jewell Parker, CEO
The Meeting Place

"I attended your 8-steps workshop in the spring. I can honestly say it changed my life. Thank you for your insight."

—Kelly Roberts, President
Ricochet Fuel Distributors, Inc.

"I've taken on a whole new way of thinking..."

"Since taking the 8-steps workshop in June, I have taken on a whole new way of thinking in regards to my business and personal life. Thank you for the fabulous presentation and for offering concrete suggestions of how to make a dream come true."

—Marguerite Kell
National Bankers Supply, Inc.

"Probably one of the most unique and successful seminars that we have sponsored is David Shepherd's 8-steps workshop. It is so different from the typical seminar..."

—Bob Gonzalez
Group Manager, Minority/Women
Business Development
Frito-Lay, Inc.

"I can't remember a workshop that scattered so many seeds that just might grow into something! Your approach is a real winner."

—Betty Jo Taylor
The Communications Department, Inc.

"I really think this is going to be a life-changing experience for me, and I don't use those words lightly."

—Mary Ann McKinley
The Newsletter Company

"It's so different..."

"Thank you so much, David. Your workshop received rave reviews and I look forward to future collaborations."

—Debbie Hurst
Executive Director
North Texas Women's Business Council

"David Shepherd has a unique ability to challenge and inspire."

—Dr. Raymond Smilor
The Kauffman Foundation

"I expect your book to do well. It's the kind of self-help combined with rock solid advice that I would buy."

—John Mitchell, Owner
The Bookcase Store

"David really knows how to engage an audience. His professionalism and presentation skills make him a star attraction."

—Jim Nolen, Sr. Lecturer
Department of Finance
The University of Texas at Austin

"This workshop was new and unique in every way."

—Leah Jones

"The changes are mind-blowing..."

"Thank you very much for an outstanding learning experience. You are a gifted speaker. And thank you for making our learning experience a rewarding and entertaining one."

—Dr. Charles R. Denham, M.D.
Health Care Concepts, Inc.

"Wow! So intense to feel that level of emotion and sincerity."

—Victor Martinez

"Definitely not the same old stuff. I have never been pushed or challenged as much in a workshop."

—Jose Lara

"Thank you for your great 8 steps. We felt you were using our business for your examples! The result has been changes including price increases of 15% and up!"

—Tom Teykl, CEO
New Systems, Inc.

"Your workshop energized me!"

—Alan Lish

"I can honestly say it changed my life..."

your business or your life

8 steps for getting all you want out of BOTH

David Shepherd

Balios Publishing
Austin • Phoenix

Published by
Balios Publishing
3607 Lucas Drive
Austin, TX 78731
512-302-0301

Shepherd, David
Your Business Or Your Life:
8 Steps For Getting All You Want Out of Both

ISBN 0-9705965-2-9
1. Small Business
2. Business Management
3. Success - Business

We never know how high we are
Till we are called to rise
And then, if we are true to plan
Our statures touch the skies.

—Emily Dickinson

Acknowledgments

I dedicate this book to the thousands of small business owners I have had the privilege to meet and work with. May you come to see and achieve your own potential greatness.

I would also like to thank my family and friends for all of their support and encouragement. I offer special thanks to my mother, sister and my sons, Cam and Ash, who have had to endure years of my lectures on the importance of never giving up. Boys, I stand by my statements. I miss the other men in my life, but only in the physical realm; they have provided most of my inspiration.

Thanks to Jim Nolen and Dr. Ernest Walker for getting me involved in the University of Texas' Community MBA program. How rewarding to have put over a thousand minority business owners through that great program. Thanks also to Jim and Dr. George Gau for recruiting me to teach entrepreneurship at UT Austin, and to Dr. Barbara Fossum for allowing me to teach in the wonderful graduate program at ICC. Also to my many Finance 374-S students at the University of Texas at Austin whose research can be found herein.

To Debbie Hurst and Bob Gonzalez., I would like say how much your early vote of confidence in my workshop has meant to me. Thank you.

Thanks also to Emily Weida for her outstanding editing work; the mistakes in this book are no doubt where I chose to ignore her advice. Thanks also to Fred Walters, publisher of Acres U.S.A., who offered much assistance, and to Bill Branson—a true friend and colleague.

There are many others to thank as well, but there are also plenty of books left in me. I'll catch up with them later.

Pareto's Law (The 80/20 Rule)

In my university classes and in my workshops, one of the first concepts I introduce is Pareto's Law, otherwise known as the 80/20 Rule.

At first, students and workshop attendees may think I am making a minor point. But before long, it becomes apparent that I believe this "law" must be an absolute core philosophy of the successful small business owner.

Pareto, an Italian economist and sociologist who lived from 1848 to 1923, sought to prove that wealth distribution followed nearly identical patterns, regardless of the nature of a country's economic system. Whether it was the United States, Russia, or a poor agrarian society, 20% of the population, he maintained, controlled 80% of the wealth.

While his theories were hotly disputed, they have also been widely applied to fields other than economics. For example, the following estimates will almost always be true in principle, if not exact.

- 20% of your sales representatives will make 80% of the sales
- 20% of your customers will produce 80% of your sales
- 20% of your employees will do 80% of the work

Naturally, the reverse is also true, meaning that 80% of your customers produce only 20% of your sales and profits. The point is that you don't have the time or resources to be all things to all people. You must work to identify those few critical customers, employees, tasks, etc. that will do the most to contribute to your overall success.

Pareto's Law has also been called the law of the trivial many and the critical few. Whenever you see the name Pareto in this book, remember, I am imploring you to become acutely aware of what truly matters and what does not, and then deal almost exclusively with the former.

Contents

Introduction

I have often thought that the best way to define a man's character would be to seek out the particular mental or moral attitude in which, when it came upon him, he felt himself most deeply and intensely active and alive. At such moments there is a voice inside which speaks and says: "This is the real me!"

—William James

First, a word about the title of this book. In defense of my age, I was very, very young when Jack Benny was on the air, but even so, he made me laugh. In one of the funniest skits I have ever seen performed on television, two burglars accost Benny. In case you're not familiar with him, I should tell you that Benny was a miser of unimaginable proportions. As an example, his home phone was a pay phone!

The burglars, anxious and hurried, issued the classic command to Benny: "Your money or your life."

To their shock, Benny said nothing. Incredibly, he appeared distant, dreamy. They repeated their demand, louder: "Your money or your life!"

Benny said nothing.

Frustrated and starting to panic, the burglars shouted their demand one final time: *"Your money or your life!"*

To which Benny, the miser, finally responded, *"I'm thinking, I'm thinking."*

Most entrepreneurs start their businesses with the expectation of building a better life for themselves and for their families. Compared to Corporate America, they may also harbor dreams of greater autonomy, independence and unlimited potential. They want to be able to set their own goals and look only to themselves for their attainment. They will not accept ceilings, glass or otherwise.

While business goals are usually expressed in business terms, such as reaching a certain level of sales or profitability, they invariably contain within them the seeds of our innermost *personal* aspirations. Achieving success in business, it is hoped, will lead to success in life. Once successful in business, the thinking goes, we will have more time to spend with our families and on our hobbies. We will have more money to fulfill our responsibilities, enhance our security and enable us to contribute to others. We will have the time and money to enjoy life.

Goals in the early stages of a business are often simple and clear. In the beginning, it may be just you and your kitchen table, and job number one is pretty clear: Survive. Which normally translates into selling something, *anything*! The second sale doubles the first and growth momentarily seems like the least of your problems. Enthusiasm and optimism reign. There is a sense of momentum generated by the growing demands placed on your time. Merely being busy can be interpreted as a measure of success.

But small businesses have a way of quickly becoming complex after this initial honeymoon period, and the complexities can overwhelm even the best of managers. With new sales, come new customers and with new customers come new problems. To solve these problems, we often hire additional people, who bring untold additional paperwork, tax filings, management issues...and their own set of additional problems. To accommodate these new people, we need more space and equipment...and why is there never enough cash?

The focus we had initially—on sales—starts to blur. We are forced to spend more and more of our time on things we don't fully understand like accounting, purchasing, operations, marketing, finance, and technology. Yet neither do we have the resources to hire experts in all of these areas, so by definition, we—the founder—end up spending more time on what we do poorly, and less time on what we do well. As our workload increases, our efficiency decreases, compounding the problem. The farther we stray from what we do best, the harder we have to work just to remain viable. This doesn't sound like a prescription for long-term success—or happiness—does it?

These complexities can become the proverbial business "tar baby." We stick one toe in the tar of administrative tasks, and that toe is stuck, week after week. Then we stick a toe in preparing payroll or a loan application. Then we stick a toe in hiring and training. Then we stick a finger in setting up a Web site. By definition, there is now less time to do other things, whether that is making a crucial sales presentation or making it to a soccer game on time.

As the hours start to fill up with…stuff…we often wish there were more hours in the day, so that we could do more…stuff. But you will not get more hours. You have the same number of hours in a week as everyone else on the planet: 168. You cannot buy, negotiate, barter or create one additional second. Of those 168 hours, 112 are typically spent awake, or 16 hours a day. Subtracting weekends (you *do* remember weekends, don't you?) you have 80 waking hours during the Monday through Friday workweek.

Which is quite a coincidence, because since a 40-hour workweek is still considered the norm, this suggests that, excluding weekends, you would ideally have 40 hours a week for your work, and 40 hours a week for your life. Half-and-half. A perfect balance.

Entrepreneurial DNA

If both halves—life and work—are working smoothly together, we could think of them as a double helix, such as that found in a molecule of DNA. The DNA molecule, literally representing life itself, is beautifully intertwined, perfectly synergistic. Now, think of one of these interconnected strands as "life," and the other as "work." It doesn't take a mathematician to determine that the more time we spend on one area of our lives, the less time we have for the remaining ones. Yet many of us seem to think that our capacity for work is unlimited. The entrepreneurial "can do" spirit that is so necessary to some aspects of running a business, invariably becomes a detriment in the area of time management—the most crucial area of all.

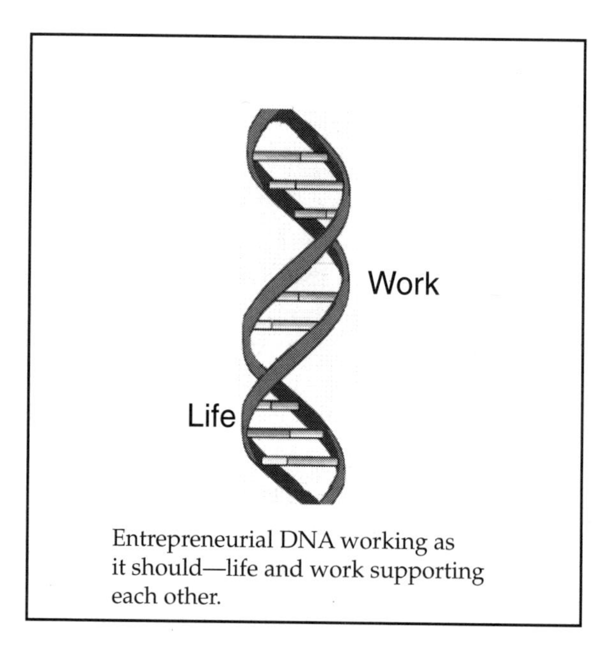

Entrepreneurial DNA working as it should—life and work supporting each other.

For those who have run their businesses for two years or more, the separation between the "strands" of business and life has probably grown wider than you would like to admit. From that simplistic, enthusiastic startup, there are now employees, customers, contracts, suppliers, debts, meetings, commitments.... I could go on, but you know what they are!

Each increase in the complexity of your business demands more of the only resource you have: time. Which indisputably leaves less time for family, health and leisure. You created a business in hopes of obtaining a certain lifestyle, but, more often than not, you have ended up sacrificing your lifestyle to support the demands of your business.

One telltale sign of spending too much time on the work "strand" of your life, is how much time you spend justifying or defending that fact. As we spend more and more time on our work, we develop a self-protective favoritism toward that strand of our life. How else could we justify working harder at the expense of other important things in our lives? We must constantly convince ourselves that it is worth it, that it matters...that it will all work out brilliantly in the end. We try to convince ourselves (and our family and friends) that our long hours and constant difficulties are not only necessary, but also heroic!

But the mathematics disputes this. Every time we invest one minute more in our work, we have one minute less for our life. They are not one and the same. The unappreciated strand ("life") will either begin to atrophy or pull apart, looking to fulfill its own more spiritual needs—some of which were the reasons we started down this self-directed path in the first place! Once separated, neither strand can remain healthy. Both begin to wither. They compete against, rather than work for, each other.

Or, in Jack Benny's terms, if someone demands of you, "Your business or your life!" you would have to respond, *"I'm thinking, I'm thinking."*

Before we can bring the two strands of your entrepreneurial DNA back into concert, let's briefly consider them individually. We'll start with the easy one—your business. What did you want out of your business when you started it? Perhaps you had some business goals that were easy to set because we almost always reduce them to numerical measures:

- I want to reach $2 million in sales. (Or $10 million or $100 million.)
- I want to have 20 locations nationwide.
- I want to pay myself $125,000 a year and build a business worth $1 million, and so on.

Studies have shown that clearly stated goals are more likely to be achieved than vague ones, so I encourage and applaud such specificity. But there was another side—a more important side—to your decision to go into business for yourself, wasn't there? It was not the issue of "what" you wanted out of your business, but "why" you wanted those things. Examining the "why," invariably leads us to the "life" half of our DNA molecule.

- I want to reach $2 million in sales *because* I can then hire a manager so that I can start traveling more.
- I want to have 20 locations nationwide *because* I want to prove I can do what that *Fortune* 500 company I used to work for didn't believe I could do.
- I want to pay myself $125,000 a year and build a business worth $1 million, *because* I want to buy a second home in Santa Fe in ten years and retire.

Why Do You Want To Succeed?

It would be an excellent idea to stop right now and write down three to five answers to the question, "When you started your own business, *why* did you want to succeed?" I ask you to think back to a simpler time, because the complexities of running a small business have a way of blurring the initial sharpness of our goals. It's hard, for example, when the veins are popping out of your forehead as you scream at your computer that just crashed, to remember that you began your business with a vision of being able to take time off to work among the butterflies in your garden.

In fact, it would be helpful if you could go back even farther—perhaps to the first time as a child that you remember setting goals for your life. There is a certain purity to the dreams we have as children, and, I believe, an enduring emotional connection. While being an astronaut, quarterback, or nurse may no longer be an option for you (or even of interest to you), the reasons *why* you once wanted those things may be as relevant and potentially inspiring today as they were when you were a child.

I wrote my first major life goal in a journal when I was only ten—to win an Olympic gold medal. That's another good thing about reaching as far back as you can; anything seemed possible when we were young. I knew it would be in track and field, but I didn't even know what event I would pursue. I found a plastic replica of a gold medal and hung it on my wall. For no particular reason, I selected the mile as my event...and then started running every day.

Influenced by my older brother, by age eleven I had switched events to the pole vault. My father even set up a crude runway and pit for us in our backyard. I did other things as I entered my teenage years, I even played other sports and dated girls from time to time. But never a day passed that I didn't think about standing atop the Olympic award stand, accepting my gold medal and singing the national anthem as I brushed tears from my eyes. Every day, I looked at that gold medal replica and took some small action (perhaps 50 push-ups or fifteen minutes of studying films) that I hoped would move me closer to my goal.

In the United States system, there is one event, the Olympic Trials, that determines the U.S. track and field team.

It is held in the summer, approximately two to three months before the Olympic Games. The top three in each event qualify. At age eleven, I managed to clear eight feet in the pole vault. The world record at that time was 16' 8". While I had no way to know it then, to make the U.S. team twelve years later, and to have a chance to compete for the gold medal, I would have to clear *eighteen* feet!

With eight years to go before the Trials, I was clearing thirteen feet. With four years to go, I was clearing fifteen feet. With two years to go, I cleared 16' 8" (coincidentally, the world record height at the time I had first set out on this journey), and with one full year to go, I cleared 17' 5". Still young and getting faster, stronger and improving in technique, I had one year left to improve a mere seven inches to make the U.S. team—an improvement that would have been the *smallest* annual improvement I had made in almost a decade.

Of course I still did other things, like completing a degree at the University of Texas at Austin, but I was so focused on pole vaulting that not an hour went by—day or night—that I wasn't thinking about it. As I walked across campus between classes, I would mentally rehearse my technique. On many days, I would workout in both the morning and the afternoon. I would watch film of the world's top vaulters until late into the night. I would imagine that victory stand and look at that plastic gold medal that still hung on my wall.

Alas, history will record that I did not win the gold medal. I didn't even make the U.S. Olympic team. In a rare concession to having some semblance of a social life, about nine months before the Trials, I joined some close friends for a tubing expedition down a Central Texas river. Seeking a quick thrill, I followed others who were riding the rapids through a narrow flume and over the top of a dam, all despite warning signs that the water below was extremely shallow.

The good news was that I only suffered a severe sprain to my right ankle. The bad news was that I shattered my left ankle. After months in a cast, the atrophy, the rehabilitation, the constant pain...The Dream was dead. I was devastated. I had devoted half my life to a goal, and now, I had failed.

Or had I? From a more mature perspective, I can now see that there were several life lessons I could draw from that ordeal. First, of course, I could have cautioned myself never to dream the Big Dream again, because too many things can go wrong—even fate can play a determining role. But there was also another interpretation. I had to admit that literally going for the gold, even starting from the perspective of a skinny ten-year-old of unknown talent, I had come tantalizingly close through sheer force of will. I had learned that even the most audacious goal, given ample time and consistent effort, might be within the reach of anyone. Wouldn't that mean that a similar commitment to a different goal could result in total victory?

And last but not least, there is the perspective that, while I had been obsessed with the ultimate goal, I had also achieved hundreds of smaller goals en route—goals that I perhaps had not stopped to properly recognize and celebrate at the time. I had set records and won championships at every grade level, I received a full scholarship to a top college, I traveled all across the United States, and was an NCAA All-American. I had learned a lifetime of lessons about the results of self-discipline and hard work.

Success or failure? It all depends on *my* definition doesn't it? But on the verge of graduating from college, my pole vaulting days behind me, it was crucial that I decide, in my own mind, which it had been. My answer would determine whether or not, at age 22, I was willing to take another big risk. Even at that young age, I knew what I wanted to do for the rest of my life: write. Only now, the need to earn a living, and pressures stemming from a family legacy of successful lawyers and businessmen, combined to prevent me from taking that big risk. Instead, I got a "real job" working for a large company, and later went back to school to earn an

MBA. After that, I started several small businesses, began consulting with other entrepreneurs, and taught at the University of Texas.

While I enjoyed certain aspects of all of these endeavors, the urge to write never left me. Each year I would sit down in January and take stock of my personal goals and achievements and not a year passed that I didn't bemoan the fact that I had found so little time to write. The little writing I did make time for, was usually an escape when things were not going well on other fronts. But, whenever I would use that escape, I would typically end up even more depressed. I would chastise myself for being unable to find a way to write for a living. In my mind, in my heart, I was a writer. The only problem was...I wasn't writing! I was too busy doing other things, like making a living.

Succeed At Being You

What, I wonder, are you...that you are not honoring? Why don't you take a few minutes and write down three to five things that you "are," but which you are not presently committing time to. I don't want to prejudice you, but these will often come from your artistic side, including things like music, poetry and painting. Or, it may include volunteerism, travel, writing, reading, working out or parenting activities. Think back to your childhood if necessary, but don't think about this for too long. Let your first reactions guide you. Use the margins of this book or a journal or a Post-it note to jot down what it is that you're doing when you feel your absolute best.

We can bury who we are and what we were meant to do for long periods of time, and the complexities of a small business often do this for us. But I do not think that we can permanently escape these truths. After 20 years of repeating this cycle of wanting to write, but not doing it, I finally snapped. Maybe it was a midlife crisis, or maybe it was the culmination of years of reinforcing my desire to write, but I finally decided the time had come. I gave up all consulting work (and all income!), rented a lake house, grew my hair long and just wrote.

Well, that's almost true. Actually, for about two months, I didn't write. I *couldn't* write! I just paced in front of the keyboard thinking about writing, and got angrier and angrier each day that I was not writing, despite, for the first time in my life, having absolutely nothing else to do. The days seemed to last for 50 hours, yet I accomplished nothing. There was a very powerful feeling within me that I had come to a point in my life where there was nothing left to do but pursue my lifetime goal, and because of that, I was scared to death to make the effort.

It was one thing to fail at selling computers, or even at pole vaulting. But what if I failed at being me? Further intensifying the problem, I have to admit, was that the outcome I had in mind was not merely to write, or even to scratch out a living by writing. Oh no, I wanted the gold medal equivalent. I wanted to write the Great American Novel. I didn't want to write a pamphlet, corporate brochure or newsletter. I wanted to write a James Clavell-caliber, 1,400-page epic that would soar to #1 on the *New York Times* Bestseller list...and I wanted it completed by noon that day! Which, when I realized it could take five years—or 25 to achieve my goal, or, that fate might never allow it, made it pretty hard to sit down and type out that first sentence. Which made me angry—angry that I hadn't started earlier, angry that I had gotten so far off track in my life, angry that I was going to have to work so hard. It made me wonder if I should give up on my goal completely. Perhaps it was too late. Perhaps audacious goals were exclusively for children and dangerous to adults.

And then I remembered the lessons of a ten-year-old gold medallist wannabe. With no possible way to determine whether his goal was achievable or not, he had simply committed to it, put a visual representation of it up on his wall, and set about working on it in small ways every day. And while he fell short of that specific goal, he received enormous rewards along the way. Given a chance to do it over again, would he change the goal? Certainly not. All he would do differently (other than *not* going tubing) would be to enjoy and celebrate the small wins that occurred along the way. He would learn to enjoy the journey, while ever hopeful of the destination.

So, in my 40s, rather than "getting real," I set the goal of writing the Great American Novel. I put a picture of James Clavell's *Shogun* where my plastic gold medal used to hang. Writing is what I want to do most and no matter how many setbacks I encounter, no matter what others may think, or how many publishers reject my work, I will spend the rest of my life doing just that. Sure, others may roll their eyes when I tell them what I am doing with my life, but *it's my life!* It's who I am and what I enjoy. Writing a great sentence is when I feel most perfect, even though I know that I can't control fate any more than I can control the rapids of a Central Texas river. I can only do the best I can do, and let the rest take care of itself.

Meanwhile, I'm going to celebrate the good things that occur along the way—this nonfiction book that you're reading, for example. Hey, only five years after committing, I have completed a novel (and have an agent!), and I'm making a living as a writer! Even if my novels never see the light of day, having them as a goal will have created a very pleasurable life for me—much more in line with my dreams than where I had been heading. I no longer stare at the keyboard for weeks at a time, but rather I sit down in a very disciplined manner six days a week and write for at least four or five hours. I've discovered that you have a much better chance of getting your books published if you've actually written them! (As opposed to just talking about writing them.) I've also discovered that you get better at things that you actually practice. Amazing, isn't it?

Don't Back Down
My life lessons have lead to this conclusion th to harness the power of your own lifetime goa words of singer Tom Petty, "don't back down." big, emotional goals are the most powerful. T pull you along and create scores of "wins" along the way, whether or not you ever reach the ultimate goal. Soichiro Honda didn't set out to create a car, he set out to create a piston ring...then a sewing machine...then a motorized bicycle....

Once you have renewed and clarified your personal lifetime goals, it becomes a much simpler matter to *link* them to your success in business. Business goals are usually expressed in money, but money alone is never enough to maintain our enthusiasm—it's the opportunities that money creates that are motivational. Our businesses should be the means, not the ends. The end is our set of lifetime goals. Money should be for a purpose and you must know what that purpose is. Your business should be the engine that creates the money and the free time necessary for you to pursue your personal lifetime goals, whether or not they are directly related to your business.

Money and time? Aren't those two things that small businesses soak up like sponges? Yes, but that is what the eight steps in this book are going to change. The eight steps in this book are going to return to you the money and the time necessary to pursue what matters most to you in life.

There will always be hard times in running your own business. There will always be demanding customers, disgruntled employees, absurd regulations, bills to pay—things that you just don't want to deal with. But the closer you can link these business activities to the accomplishment of your lifetime goals, the more trivial these and other distasteful tasks will seem. When you constantly keep your lifetime goals in mind, and have a specific plan for your business to serve as the engine of attainment, everything you have to do suddenly matters.

This is not a book about setting goals. This is not a book intentionally designed to motivate you. Books like that exist by the thousands. The problem with many of them, in my opinion, is that they fail to provide the specific tools necessary, not just to set the goals (that's easy), but to develop a step-by-step plan for generating the money and the time necessary to attain those goals. Dreams cost money and goals worth reaching take time.

Mapping Your Life

For I dipped into the future, far as
human eye could see,
Saw the Vision of the world, and all
the wonder that would be.

—Alfred, Lord Tennyson

Where do you want to go in your life, and why? Even if you start with broad generalities, the answers to these crucial questions can serve as a map for getting there. I have always found a map to be the perfect metaphor in the university classes I teach on competitive strategy. In the first class each semester, I display an overhead containing a segment of a road map. I then ask the question, "How do I get there?" After some head scratching (simple questions are often the toughest) someone will usually say, "Where do you want to go?"

Aha! To benefit from a map, it would help to know where you want to go. I then pick out a town—St. Cloud, Minnesota in most cases—and repeat my question: "How do I get there?" Again a pause, and finally, "Where are you starting from?"

Aha! To benefit from a map, it would help to know both where you want to go, and where you are now. If you know those two things, you can then use the map to devise a variety of routes, based on such things as your resources (car, bike...donkey?) and your desires (speed, sightseeing, shopping?). A business plan, or even back-of-a-napkin projections, usually provides the "map" for our business goals. For example, you may want to do $500,000 in sales this year, $1,000,000 next year, $3,000,000 in five years...all with a 7% after-tax profit margin.

But what about a map for our lives—the other half of our entrepreneurial DNA? What are the crucial measures when it comes to matters of the heart and soul? How do we quantify them? How do we measure them? How do we depict them so that we can use them as motivation toward our success? And how do we link them to our efforts at work so that the two strands complement, rather than compete against, each other?

I've already mentioned a method that has worked powerfully me and for many others. Do you remember my plastic gold medal? How about the picture of the book *Shogun* that now hangs on my wall? I would like to formally introduce this method to you now, and encourage you to experiment with it as you implement the 8 steps.

Creating what I call a photo map is not necessary for using the 8 steps to improve your business performance. It is, however, necessary for linking the improved performance of your business to the attainment of important lifetime goals. The results of those who have used this process in my workshops are often profound. I urge you to take it seriously and give it a try.

Creating a Photo Map

A photo map is simply a series of photographs or images that visually represent where you want to be in your life at some point in the future. A photo map is a collage of images jointly depicting what matters most to you—that which you are working toward. That which makes work worthwhile.

A photo map harnesses the most powerful goal-setting techniques that have been proven over time to work. These methods have worked for millions of people, they have worked for centuries, they have worked for 8-steps workshop graduates, and, though scientists are unsure as to precisely how or why they work...they will work for you!

To give you an example, I would like for you to imagine one of your fondest—or perhaps saddest—family photographs. If it's nearby, get it in your hands. Perhaps it's one of you as a child, bringing back memories of innocence and possibilities. Or, perhaps it's one of a sibling who has passed away, or a child who has excelled. Photographs such as these can instantly change our emotions, bringing such reactions as laughter, anger or tears.

If we were to write out, in great detail, the *reasons* that these photographs evoke such strong reactions, we would no doubt be writing for a long, long time. A woman who cries over the picture of her daughter in cap and gown, or a wedding dress, is not reacting simply to that event; she is reacting to a series of events far more profound and complex. Hypothetically, when she views that photograph, she could be thinking about the day she first met her husband, her difficult pregnancy, the trips to the emergency room, and the endless parade of her daughter's soccer games, boyfriends and myriad other challenges. One powerful image invokes dozens, or perhaps thousands, of others.

If asked to write down what it is that makes this photograph so meaningful, she very well might write hundreds of pages. If the photograph was then destroyed, her only way to evoke these same emotions would be to invest hours in reading through those pages, and even then it is doubtful that the effect would be remotely as strong. While words could require hours (which we do not have to spare) to summon the proper combination of emotions, the photograph can do so with but a glance lasting no more than a millisecond. Her brain has already hard-wired those hundreds of pages to the single image, and, faster than any computer ever could, can process them instantly. You may be thinking that I've just described that old expression, "a picture is worth a thousand words." Change thousand to million, and I'll agree with you.

The process of photo mapping is as simple as it is powerful. It harnesses the instant, visceral power of visual images, to the classic strategic metaphor of a map—that is, a guide for getting us where we want to go. It is also extremely enjoyable.

A Photo Map

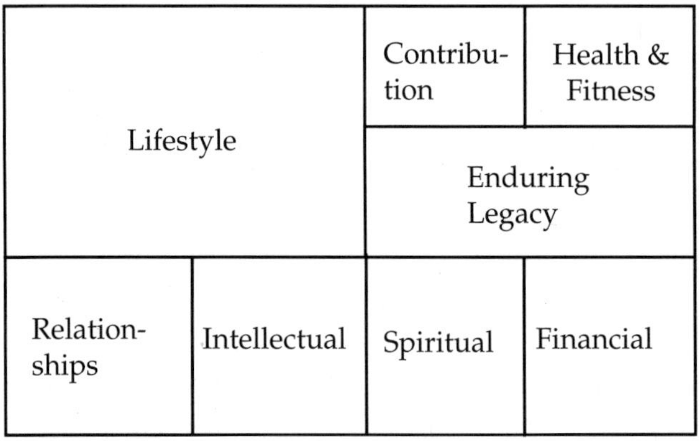

<table>
<tr><td colspan="2" rowspan="2">Lifestyle</td><td>Contribution</td><td>Health & Fitness</td></tr>
<tr><td colspan="2">Enduring Legacy</td></tr>
<tr><td>Relationships</td><td>Intellectual</td><td>Spiritual</td><td>Financial</td></tr>
</table>

Here's one popular format for photo maps. The point is to find images representing how you would like your life to be in each of these areas, say 5-10 years from now. I would show acctual ones, but black and white printing does not do them justice. Please go to www.8steps.net to see color photo maps.

I have developed a photo map template that contains eight separate image areas. After years of evaluating this process and studying myriad other approaches, I believe these eight cover the things that most of us worry about and would like to see fulfilled in our lives. Trying to work with images that are motivational, but reachable, I normally use a time horizon of 5-10 years for photo map purposes. You can experiment with shorter or longer time horizons until you find that which works best for you. Also, feel free to tweak the categories so that they make the most sense to you.

The eight areas I concentrate on are as follows. Note that the first letter of each forms the acronym RICHES FL, which I remember as "RICHES For Life." As a source of images, magazines, Internet sites, stock photography, etc., can prove just as valuable as personal photo collections. (Most photo maps include color photographs; a black and white reproduction simply does not do them justice. If you would like to see samples of actual photo maps, please go to www.8steps.net.)

R Relationships. What relationships will you value, or do you seek, at some point in the future? This may include a closer bond with people you've loved forever, or new relationships with people you've yet to meet. Think of how you can depict loving and supportive relationships with a visual image.

I Intellectual. Every study finds that the way to keep our minds sharp into old age is to keep them engaged. What image represents your commitment to yourself to pursue a lifetime of learning and intellectual challenges?

C Contribution. Helping others less fortunate than us enriches every aspect of our lives. What will you be doing five to ten years from now to make a difference in the lives of others?

H Health & Fitness. Nothing else on your photo map will matter if you're not healthy enough to enjoy it. And, if you're not healthy, you can quickly become a burden for others. So, not only for yourself, but also for the sake of those you care about, health must come first.

E **Enduring Legacy.** What will others say about you when you're gone? What would you like for them to say? Write your own brief epitaph and find an image to convey it.

S **Spirituality.** Most of us believe in something greater than ourselves, but just where do you want to be, later in life, in terms of understanding the meaning of it all?

F **Financial.** This will be addressed throughout this book, but there's no harm in finding an image that depicts the level of financial security you desire. For some this image may be a rustic cabin in the woods, while for others it may be a private jet.

L **Lifestyle.** The challenge here is to find one unifying image that, in your mind, represents a fulfilling and enjoyable life, including advancement in the other seven photo map areas. More on this in a moment.

Reasons To Succeed

Another thing that we know about setting goals—or better yet about achieving them—is that the more *reasons* we have for wanting to succeed, the more likely we are to succeed. Tony Robbins is one who advocates this approach, saying in effect that if you can find enough reasons *why* you want to accomplish something, you will find the "how."

As you look at your "best self" as depicted by your photo map images, list some reasons *why* you want to be that person. Also, tell yourself the "story" of those images. Remember the hypothetical exercise where I said the woman could write a book based on one picture? By telling yourself the story of a particular image, you're effectively reversing that procedure. You are taking your thoughts, memories and words, and ascribing the emotions you feel to the image you have selected. Think of that image as some sort of memory chip into which you are downloading all of the data that you want that chip to permanently store and instantly recall.

Once you've spent just a few moments doing this with each image, you'll never have to do it again. From that point forward, you will have empowered that particular image with the ability to tell its story—complete with all reasons and emotions—in a millisecond. Just glancing at the image can infuse you with hope, optimism and, most importantly, daily determination. I will leave it to you to imagine the power of glancing at such a powerful image not just once, but perhaps ten, fifty…or thousands of times a day! We do indeed become what we think about all day, just as every great thinker from Jesus to Buddha to Emerson has tried to tell us.

Remember the lifestyle image from above? For this image, many people chose a house, or a piece of land that they imagine themselves living on in the future. Others have chosen images ranging from luxury resorts to empty beaches, to porches filled with grandchildren. It's up to you. What I suggest, however, is that once all of your images are selected (and feel free to change them anytime something more powerful catches your eye), you repeat the process from above and ascribe all of your individual image goals to the single lifestyle image. For example, someone with an Intellectual goal of reading 50 books a year, and a Health & Fitness goal of working out four days a week, could imagine a "dream house" with a library and a gym inside. This would enable a single image—the house—to instantly evoke multiple photo map emotions.

While today's scanning technology makes it simple to create a photo map complete with all eight images, and to quickly reproduce this montage in many formats (from a poster or wallet-sized picture to a screen saver) it can also simplify things to have one dominant image—the lifestyle image. I keep a complete photo map on a wall near where I work, but I also keep just the singular lifestyle image in my wallet and on my computer screen saver. After going through the exercises described above, I can glance at that one image (a house in Santa Fe) for only a second, and not only imagine myself there, but imagine myself having made great progress toward all seven other photo map goals. It's a quick and powerful way to refocus my efforts on the task that will make the greatest contribution toward getting me where I want to go—to following my photo map.

Without a tool like the photo map to keep our priorities constantly in front of us, the world will overwhelm our ability to manage our time. Reuters News Service reports that more information has been created in the past 30 years than in the previous five thousand, and that rate is accelerating. All of the information created in the history of the world is now doubling every five years. Pages of information on the World Wide Web are being measured in billions. To provide a context for these astounding numbers, a million seconds passes in about eleven and a half days while a billion seconds takes almost 32 years.

And it's not just the Internet that is overwhelming us. To add to our overload, we have cellular phones (in our cars, in our pockets, in our golf carts, at our children's soccer games), pagers, call-waiting, phones on airplanes, faxes, e-mail, a hundred cable channels, video-conferencing, electronic organizers, networked calendars....

The evolution of information, driven by technology's ability to handle it, is growing at exponential rates and humans have no hope of keeping up. W. Brian Arthur, Citibank Professor at the Santa Fe Institute, wrote an article for *Scientific American* in which he estimated technology was evolving at a rate roughly ten million times the speed of natural human evolution. *Ten million!*

No wonder a recent poll reported that 61% of managers had cancelled social engagements because of information overload and two-thirds said that in trying to keep up with all the information they feel they *must* read, they often find themselves too tired for leisure activities. If there is one legacy of the American worker during the early stages of the information era, that may well be it: Too tired for leisure! So much for the lifestyle benefits promised by automation.

For too many of us, being busy has become a surrogate for being productive. Getting things done is no longer as important as simply doing things. Activity, no matter how trivial, is today's anesthesia for the pain of mediocrity. And the electronic era has made it easy to feel busy since we may be reached 24 hours a day in almost every corner of the world. Most of us allow not just one person, but many, to interrupt our schedules, our priorities and our progress toward our personal goals.

If you are not where you want to be in your life, I believe the reason is that you have not vigorously defended the time to do what matters most to you. Whether or not you choose to harness the power of the photo map, if you really want to achieve more in your business and your life, then you must dedicate more of your time to activities directly related to your lifetime goals.

This book is about having both a business and a life—a business worth living for, and a lifestyle worth working toward. It lays out a powerful process that has proven effective for entrepreneurs in all types of business, all across the country. This book is about developing goals and employing specific business tools that will heal the rift, that will reconnect the disparate strands of your entrepreneurial DNA so that your business and your life become healthy proponents of each other.

Overcoming Resource Poverty

Harvard professor Amar Bhide describes the challenge facing entrepreneurs as "resource poverty." While we must deal with the same operational, managerial, financial and regulatory issues as, say, General Electric, we cannot afford to hire experts in all of these areas. Nor do we have ready access to capital markets. The only resource that you, as CEO of your company, have in identical proportions to the CEO of GE, is time.

Time is all you have. Period. It's your only natural resource, and how you allocate your time will be the sole determinant of whether you succeed or fail—as you define those terms. The 8 steps seek to show you where to spend you time if you want to become your best self.

The 8 steps all share certain attributes. They have all passed through high-level filters and have been successfully implemented by thousands. I probably could have listed *800* steps based on my 20 years of working with thousands of small business owners, running my own businesses and teaching college courses. But I knew that my challenge was to select only those few tools that would meet the needs and demands of today's entrepreneur. These 8 steps are proven winners and they all share the following characteristics:

• Each step is pragmatic, straightforward and can be easily implemented by the typical business owner who is not only busy but may also lack any formal business education;

• The steps follow a philosophy of less is more, resulting in a streamlined business model, replacing complexity with a more profitable and enjoyable simplicity;

• The payoff from each step comes quickly, providing the necessary incentive and encouragement for the business owner to keep going;

• The steps are *not* just more of the same. They come from areas that are often misunderstood or underutilized and areas that are not often found in books for small business owners;

• While the steps can stand alone, they may also work together such that implementing all eight "tells the story" of how business and lifetime goals can be linked and simultaneously achieved.

This is a book about achieving your lifetime personal goals through small business ownership. It is about linking life and work in a manner that makes them both more successful (as *you* define success), more fulfilling and more fun. Most important, it is a book about making sure that what you are doing today leads directly and surely to where you want to be tomorrow.

And it is a book about the fact that it is *never* too late to set Big Goals. I recently began taking piano lessons from a teacher who specializes in adult beginners and who knows what we are all thinking deep inside. Over her piano hangs this sign:

> How old will you be when you can finally play? The same age you will be if you can't. The choice is yours.

The only decision the piano student has to make is whether or not it is worth it to them to commit the time, recognizing that time spent at the piano is time taken from somewhere else. This holds true for everything you hope to accomplish. You can have whatever you want if you're willing to commit the time. How old will you be when you achieve all of the goals depicted on your photo map? That's right, the same age you will be if you don't devote the time.

Sure, we all experience moments of doubt and uncertainty—moments when we wonder if we should have taken the self-directed path at all. Perhaps there are moments when we add up the foregone benefits we would have accrued by now if we had worked for a big company. We may sometimes wonder if we have what it takes to get over the proverbial hump. We may worry about whether technology, cash, lawsuits or myriad other threats will do us in. We may fret over what effects the relentless demands of our business are having on our social and family lives.

Sometimes the road *more* traveled looks darn appealing! Most entrepreneurs are goal-oriented, but they are sometimes so overwhelmed by day-to-day issues that they lose sight of their once inspirational long-term goals. They sometimes look back and wonder if they've made any progress at all. They agonize that there is never enough cash, even for those with growing sales, and they worry that they may not have the money to retire that they had hoped for, much less the money to fund their once glamorous lifestyle fantasies.

If You Can Survive, You Can Thrive

But it is not too late. This book will prove to you that if you can survive in business, you can thrive. If you have what it takes to hang on, then you have what it takes to move your business—and your life—to the next level. The difference is almost always razor thin. Success on a major scale will not require radical surgery, just a few nips and tucks. The very same fortitude and perseverance that has enabled you to hang on despite all obstacles, will push you over the top when properly channeled.

If you employ all of the 8 steps, you will be rewarded with a profound and positive impact on your business and your life. I hope you will use them all. But the difference between a struggling business and a thriving business is often so small, that even *one* of the 8 steps may turn your business around almost instantly. And when the turnaround comes, it will come not like a fine mist, but like a tsunami, washing over you at a rate you can hardly imagine.

Entrepreneurship is not so much a chosen profession as a way of being. It is not what we do, but who we are. We have chosen, or been called, to express who we are through our work. Jobs are to meet material needs; entrepreneurship meets the needs of the soul. You do not need to suffer in order to enjoy the rewards of independence and autonomy. If you can survive, you can thrive.

We all want the same basic things out of business ownership. We want to feel that what we do makes a difference, that we are at least competent at it (if not terrific), and we want to be well compensated. Okay...we want to be rich, but rich must be defined in more than purely financial terms.

One form of richness is to enjoy life. Truly successful entrepreneurs bring enthusiasm to their work. In order to achieve sustained profitability and create permanent wealth, you must bring enthusiasm to your work. And, in order to be enthusiastic at work, you *must* see that your efforts are creating the wealth that will take you where you want to go in your life.

I Am One Of You

To fully understand *my* passion for *your* journey, I'd like to remind you, that even though I have most recently served on the faculty of one of the top-ranked business schools in the world, most of my life has been spent as an entrepreneur. As I speak to business owners across the nation, I tell them that it is not my academic credentials that qualify me to be in front of them; it is the fact that I have paced my office late at night, wondering how I would make payroll the next day!

Yes, first and foremost, I am one of you, and that is the perspective from which I write. My advice is based on some of the most advanced and proven techniques taught in the nation's top business schools, but I will only present this information to you if I can do so in a practical manner that you can implement and benefit from immediately. The serious solutions in this book do not require new hardware, software, complex systems or high-priced consultants. All I'm asking for you to do is invest a few hours applying the powerful tools.

If time is your only vital resource, then deciding where to invest your time is your only vital decision for success. The 8 steps are the culmination of all of my experiences, which have led to my recommendations for how you should spend your time. Implementing the 8 steps will, I am confident, be the best investment of your time that you can make.

I congratulate you for acquiring this book. I've been in your shoes and I pledge to you that there is not a word in it that is not respectful of your time. Read it. Use it.

And then, when presented with the choice of, "Your business or your life!" instead of responding, "I'm thinking, I'm thinking...," you can confidently respond: "Both!"

Preparing For Change

Things Do Not Change; We Change

—Henry David Thoreau

By definition, if your business and your life are not exactly where you would like for them to be, you'll have to do some things differently. Whether you are stuck, drifting, backsliding or just not progressing as desired, certain changes will be necessary to put you on the right track.

The first and most critical change will invariably be mastering the art of change itself. Without understanding, on a conscious level, the myriad barriers to change, the environment necessary to implement the 8 steps in this book will be absent. In other words, while each of the 8 steps can stand alone, without mastering the art of change, the benefits you stand to gain from the remainder of the book will pale in comparison to what they could be.

In this first step, you will be exposed to case studies in which astonishing positive results have been achieved through a company's ability to consistently implement changes. You will see that even the smallest changes can have dramatic results. And, they can be fun. At the end of this step, I hope you will no longer view change as a necessary evil to be avoided at all costs, but rather as a powerful management philosophy to be embraced for great gain.

I have already congratulated you for surviving in business. That's the hard part, and that's why I know that if you can survive, you can thrive. But I would go further than that and say not only *can* you thrive, but that you *must* thrive! Remaining in survival mode for too long can also be described as being stuck. Without change, there are only two types of businesses—those that are stuck and those that are going to get stuck. And once stuck, powerful human emotions kick in that work to keep us stuck; it is these unconscious emotions, sometimes called the "comfort zone," that we must become aware of and consciously overcome.

Once we've reached a place of survival, the natural human reaction is to stop taking risks, to stop changing. This is supported by Abraham Maslow's famous hierarchy of human needs, which states that humans will fight hardest for such essentials as food, shelter and safety, but will risk less and less for desirable goals higher up in the hierarchy. Risking means giving up something known for something unknown and humans are not well suited for that. We like our comfort zones, no matter how marginal, which psychologists tell us is why some people stay in abusive and harmful relationships. They would rather be abused than face the risk of change, no matter how much better the potential outcome *might* be. It's the lack of certainty that drives us crazy. Some entrepreneurs are being abused by their own companies.

Intolerable vs. Irresistible

The only two circumstances under which we will take the risks necessary to change are when our present situation becomes intolerable or our dreams of the future become irresistible. The interesting thing is that both of these variables—our present situation and our future goals—are completely subjective. Did I succeed as a pole vaulter, or did I fail? That depends on my viewpoint and my definition, doesn't it? If your most recent goal has been to merely pay your bills, and you've been successful doing that, then you might believe that your present situation is tolerable. If, however, your most recent goals include visions of your kids in college, an annual family reunion on a Hawaiian beach, and a home with a view...the identical present financial situation would be wholly intolerable.

The facts are the same, but the conclusion is completely different based on a subjective interpretation of your life goals. Whether or not your present situation is tolerable or intolerable can only be answered in terms of, "relative to what?" I'm urging you, for the purpose of employing the tools in this book, to describe your present situation as relative to where you want to be in 5-10 years. Just as you can describe a glass as either half full or half empty, you can describe your daily routine as either tolerable or intolerable. And, you can describe your plans for the future in either a ho-hum manner, or in a manner that is dramatic and compelling. The choice is yours, but beware of the temptation to lower future expectations in order to meet present reality, instead of raising future expectations in order to meet lifetime goals. Most of us have had great dreams for our futures at some point in our lives, but the insidious nature of the comfort zone can infect our minds over time with these poor substitutes for the drivers of change:

- Things are not so bad the way they are now, they could be worse;
- I shouldn't aim too high because I might be disappointed;
- I'm willing to take risks to achieve my goals...I just need to wait a few months until this current crisis passes;
- If things haven't changed by now, they never will.

Welcome Discomfort

Almost invariably, when we take risks and make changes, we feel a sense of discomfort. The greater the risk, the greater the discomfort. That discomfort stems from your inner voice harping on the risks of creating a better life for you. The battleground is your willingness to adopt change as a management (and personal) philosophy. If the changes don't create discomfort, they're not changes likely to have a meaningful impact.

Peter Drucker, perhaps the most influential management author of the 20th century, goes so far as to say that the essential, if not the only role of the business leader, is to lead change. He makes it clear that failure to do so, will lead to failure. Period. Yet change is extraordinarily difficult for most of us. It doesn't come naturally. The greatest human fear is the fear of loss. We will fight harder to protect that which we already possess (surviving) than we will to obtain something new (thriving), no matter how much better or exciting the "new" may potentially be. In the business environment, this means we utilize most of our resources—human and financial—to protect and defend that which we worked so hard to obtain. In other words, we work to protect and defend the past, when change relates to tomorrow, which quite obviously is where future profits lie. If our best and brightest employees are focused on our past, who is looking out for our future? If all of our guard is to the rear of our castle, who will warn of the hoards approaching from the front? (And they approach faster today than ever before.)

If you're like me, you've probably read dozens of times that the two biggest reasons for small business failure are a lack of capital and a lack of planning. I disagree. I believe the #1 reason for business failure is the inability of management to force change. Change, like any other management practice, can be learned and adopted as a management philosophy. If you can adopt a new billing system, or customer database program, or a new report for your sales force, you can institutionalize change. Change can, and must, become an everyday part of your company's culture.

The laws of physics tell us that the gentlest nudge (change) will set and keep an object in motion *forever*...in the absence of friction. But the world of business is far from frictionless. We are besieged every moment of every day by the friction of competition, new technologies, dissatisfied customers, employee defections, quality problems and more. If gliding through space is a frictionless environment, business on Earth is more like slogging through quicksand. Thus, it takes *continuous* effort and *continuous* change to succeed, and if you're not consciously making the effort, rest assured that your business is being dragged down and will eventually stagnate.

Celebrate Small Wins

To keep your business moving and growing, you do not have to introduce huge, radical changes. In fact, while big changes are sometimes necessary, small changes are actually preferable. Small changes can make huge differences, so long as we understand that with so much friction in the world of business, we have to constantly keep nudging to keep the "object" in motion.

The essential element of Step 1, then, is to introduce a culture of *constant* small changes into your company. This is the culture that sets the table for larger changes, even before you know what those changes might be. We learn to practice change so that we are "in shape" when the radical opportunities present themselves. We run every day so that we will be ready for the marathon. We train as a fighter trains, because, while we may not know who the next opponent will be, we know there will be one. We become an agile, adaptive firm. Small changes become small wins (which we acknowledge and celebrate) and small wins give us a sense of growth and confidence. Small changes prevent us from getting stuck. These incremental changes lead us to what

Drucker calls "crucibles" or what Andrew Grove, the longtime chairman of the Intel Corporation, calls "inflection points." These are places where giant leaps are possible, perhaps even unavoidable. But if we come to the crucible and are not prepared—because we're incapable of change, because we are rigidly trying to hang onto the past—we're unlikely to survive the future.

A great example of this is the venerable Encyclopædia Britannica Company. Started in 1768 by three Scottish printers, this company produces the most comprehensive and most highly regarded set of knowledge books in the world. By 1990, Britannica's appeal to parents to "do the right thing" for their children, had resulted in a company with $650 million in sales, great profit margins and a dominant market share. Their lifetime culture of selling door-to-door had worked for centuries, and clearly, a staid old management team saw no reason to change a good thing.

And then the bottom dropped out. After more than 200 years of growth, Britannica's sales suddenly went into a free fall, finally stabilizing at a paltry 20% of previous levels. What happened? How was this possible?

It was possible because Britannica was a company that had been in a comfort zone for so long that it proved incapable of change when an "inflection point" rattled their industry. Instead of being open to change when they first learned that Microsoft was putting an inferior encyclopedia set onto a CD-ROM called Encarta, they belittled the effort and kept knocking on doors. When the parents answering those doors began to explain that they were "doing the right thing" spending their money not on books but on computers (and getting a free copy of Encarta along the way), Britannica's sales reps ignored that line of reasoning and kept knocking on doors. Even after sales had plummeted, and Britannica was finally forced to put their own content on a CD, they priced it at $1,000—completely out of touch with the marketplace—so that their huge commissioned sales force could keep knocking on doors.

In an era when so-called dot-com companies were spending tens of millions of dollars to establish a brand name, Britannica had a name potentially worth billions. It was solid gold. If their leadership had had the flexibility to react...*they* could have done the deal with Microsoft. They could have done joint ventures with anyone they had chosen. They could have been THE knowledge portal to the Web. They might even have been Yahoo!—or more.

Instead, rather than risk the discomfort of questioning old ways they chose to keep the blinders on and to keep knocking on doors. One can only wonder how comfortable they were as they watched their 200-year-old business wither away. And paradoxically, most of the door-to-door sales jobs that they tried to protect at so high a cost, are now gone.

Boosting Productivity

The power of small changes has been studied by researchers and proven in experiments. One of the most famous is the "Hawthorne Experiments," conducted by Elton Mayo beginning in 1927. Using employees at the Western Electric Hawthorne Works in Chicago, Mayo's goal was to try to measure the effect of environmental changes on human productivity.

The workers Mayo studied worked on a piece-rate basis and productivity could thus be easily measured. One of the early changes Mayo introduced was giving the workers a five-minute rest break every hour. Despite this reduction in total time on the job, overall productivity went up. Intrigued, Mayo introduced a second five-minute break, and despite this subsequent reduction of time on the job, productivity went up again! Mayo then awarded the employees a lunch break. Can you guess what happened to productivity? Yes, it went up. He let the workers go home early on Fridays and overall productivity of the group rose. Branching out, Mayo experimented with changes in temperature and humidity. And in the process, he discovered something extraordinary, which you can put to work for your company today. After virtually every change he made, productivity went up. So did morale.

Let me now put your management skills to the test. After you read the following question, stop for a moment and think through your answer. In your own mind, form an explanation for your answer, and then continue reading to compare your answer to the actual interpretations.

Question: What do you suppose happened, when all at once, Mayo revoked *every* perk—the lunch, the breaks, everything—that he had previously extended?

Do you have your answer in mind? Did the workers revolt? Did they fall into depression causing output to plummet?

No. Yet again, productivity soared! The workers produced more output in the same number of hours than they had ever done before. Morale remained high and absenteeism was slashed. Please stop and think about this for just a moment. As a manager, can you come up with a theory to explain these counterintuitive results? There are actually a variety of theories. One contends that the Hawthorne Experiments prove that the mere act of management *paying attention* to workers increases their output and that almost any change, good or bad, equates to "paying attention."

Another theory holds that by treating the workers not as individuals, but as a group, the workers came together as a team, creating a powerful synergy in which the whole was more productive than the sum of its parts. This theory suggests that during the five-minute breaks, and later at lunch, workers got to know each other, bonded, and were able to trade "best practices" so that the poorest workers learned the methods of the best. This camaraderie was also held to be responsible for a huge decline in absenteeism (80%) that clearly provided a big boost to net output. This theory makes a great deal of sense to me.

The third theory combines elements of the first two, and I have further added my own interpretation to it, based on my observation of thousands of small businesses. This theory suggests that the mere act of change (which invariably implies that more change is on the way) shakes people out of their comfort zones and causes improvements in productivity. And the Hawthorne Experiments indicate that virtually *any* change will do.

You've no doubt heard the expression "paralysis of analysis" used to describe the situation where a manager is incapable of making a decision because he or she wants enough information to make the *perfect* decision. What the Hawthorne Effect says is that there are no perfect decisions, and the only good decisions are those that are implemented. I believe this. As a consultant, there have been many times when I have quietly listened as clients debated among themselves whether or not to accept my recommendations. I always hoped that they would, not because I was 100% sure that my recommendations were ideal, but because I was 100% sure that doing *anything* to shake up their company would help them.

Tension In The Tank

There needs to be some positive tension among your employees. I am reminded of the story of a company that was trying to ship fresh fish from the West Coast to the East Coast. They spent $100,000 to build a fresh water tank to go inside a transport plane. Yet, at the end of the ten hour flight in this propeller-driven plane, many of the fish had died and even those that survived were not very "fresh" by the time they were served.

The distraught CEO sought the advice of a marine biologist who offered a simple solution: Put a few small sharks in the tank. Not enough to do any real monetary damage, but enough to get the attention of the fish. Enough to put a little "tension in the tank." It worked. When sharks accompanied the fish on their ten-hour flight, the fish were bright-eyed and fresh upon arrival at the opposite coast. All it took was the proper incentive to encourage the fish to pay attention.

The mere act of change inevitably introduces positive tension into your company's "tank." When you think about it, there is both humor and hope in this truth. The humorous part is in imagining managers who make tough decisions, sitting back and puffing victory cigars when those decisions yield positive results. No doubt convinced that they made the "right" choice, the truth is that there may have been no "wrong" choice, that at least in the short term, almost *any* change would have increased productivity. That is the hopeful part—that it is the act of changing that matters more than the quality of thought behind the change.

Daniel Leonhardt, CEO of a $1.5 million company that makes steel plating, lost his polishing foreman—a key manager. But instead of replacing him, Leonhardt let the polishing department run itself by committee. Revenues shot up 25%! While this was included in *Inc.* magazine as an example of an innovative management decision, I'm not sure Elton Mayo would have agreed. I think Mayo might have contended that Leonhardt would have had similar results if he had managed the department himself, or brought in a tyrant to run it. Mayo might have argued that it was the change—the destruction of comfort zones and the fostering of team building—that mattered. What mattered was that Leonhardt made *a* decision, not that he made *the right* decision.

As for the impact of change on teambuilding, Freud tells us that when individuals are under stress, a group consciousness forms that is separate from that of the individuals in the group. Keep this in mind when assessing the value of change: Change creates a company consciousness and builds teams—teams that are more powerful than the sum of the individuals. Now that's leverage!

LLG, a CPA practice in Northbrook, Illinois, took change a bit farther than most, but did so in small increments. Little by little, they changed their traditional, staid CPA firm into a creative wonder. From drab offices, they evolved to furniture on wheels and a nomadic environment where everyone works from a new spot everyday. Rather than the traditional Oriental rug, they have a miniature golf course. Rather than classic works of art in the lobby, they have a huge abacus. And oh yes, since they began their change crusade, they have also doubled client referrals and tripled net income.

Turn-around consultants are notorious for making small, but very visible changes on their first day on the job. They may paint out the executives' reserved parking spaces, or cut down signs that tell people where to go or how to act. They may ceremoniously burn a procedures manual or employee handbook. They may turn a break room into a training room, or a training room into a break room. They may replace worn-out carpet or paint a dingy wall a bright color. All of this is simply a part of the psychology of communicating that things are getting ready to change, even if the precise direction of the change is as yet unknown.

Ross Perot once thought that this philosophy of change would work even at big companies. When he was first named to the Board of Directors of General Motors, he decided to mess with the executives' comfort zones. First, he suggested they get rid of the coveted heated parking garages for senior executives or at least open them up to all workers. The executives thought it over, thought about their comfortable parking spaces, thought about Detroit winters, and decided that it was a much better idea to get rid of Ross Perot. Which they did for hundreds of millions of dollars. Now that's what I call a comfort zone!

I know there are some who will think that if small changes are good, then huge changes must be great. Not so. Humans perform better with a degree of tension and pressure, but excesses of these can quickly lead to negative effects. If a given goal can be attained through ten small changes, or one big one, the ten small changes will put less strain on your employees and leave them with more gas in their tanks to pursue follow-up goals. When we accomplish huge goals, without interim stops along the way, we are often left exhausted, glad that it is over and anxious for a break. When we complete small goals, we become energized and look forward to our daily habit of small wins, small wins, small wins....

Start introducing changes into your business immediately, but keep them small. Make up a list and write down at least one change per day for the next week and record it on your calendar. Start creating a culture of change in your company today and don't ever stop. Have fun with the changes. Make them playful. Start small and keep track of the changes. (A journal to follow the implementation of all of the 8 steps is a great idea!)

Get Your Tape Measure Out

Get a new coffeepot. Paint a wall. (Paint it together with your team.) Replace that stained carpet. Move the desks around. You don't have to explain the changes, nor do you have to answer the certain-to-be-asked questions about "What's going on?" One manager I know waits until his employees are on the phone and then walks into their offices with a tape measure. As a panicked look sweeps over the employee's face, he quietly signals them to ignore him as he carefully measures the dimensions of their office. He swears that productivity surges for at least three weeks after each measuring! Which tells us that even the *prospect* of change can create a positive tension and improve productivity.

Another 8-steps workshop graduate replaced a clock in his lobby that hadn't worked in three years. He had to admit that he was shocked at how every employee commented on it the first day. Several read into it crazy things, such as he might be getting ready to sell the business. Good! Wake them up and shake them up!

Small changes can redirect our focus, and perhaps no guiding principle in this book is more important than this one: It doesn't matter where you've been, only which direction you are heading...and you can change direction in an instant. You change direction instantly by making small changes.

Sharing these small changes, and small wins, can be an excellent and powerful way to open weekly company meetings. Later in this book I will introduce the psychological principle of "set." This is the scientific explanation for what almost every great thinker in history has pronounced—we become what we think about all day. The process of announcing and recording your small changes and small wins, forces (in a good way) you and your employees to focus on the positive, building momentum that will take you steadily toward your goals.

Might you meet a little resistance as you introduce change into your company? Of course! As I said, humans naturally resist change. We don't like uncertainty, but the fact is that we perform better with a tolerable amount of it hanging over us. Learning to change is an essential ingredient to building momentum in your business. Learning to change is the antivenin for getting stuck, for failing. Introducing a culture of constant small changes is the way to prepare for the future, so that small threats are dealt with when they're small, rather than allowing them to well up on the horizon to gargantuan and fatal proportions.

If you don't introduce and maintain a culture of constant small changes into your organization, your business will eventually stall and fail. Sadly, many business owners fear change *worse* than they fear total failure, and sit helplessly by and watch as their own income declines from year to year. And, when it declines to a point they can no longer tolerate, they suddenly *spring* into action, invoking some monumental change...far too late to do any good.

Rather than look at where your business is today, pay particular attention to where it is heading. What are the trends? And don't be afraid to be an alarmist. If you're not constantly changing your organization, you should be alarmed. If, for example, you haven't really moved down the e-commerce trail, don't ask yourself whether that is hurting you today, ask yourself whether it will hurt you five years from now. When (not if) the day comes that all of your suppliers and customers will only do business with e-compatible firms, what effect will that have on you if you remain where you are today?

If the answer is that you will be out of business, then start today with small changes and small wins. If you've been selling 1,000 cases of bottled water a month, you don't need to hold a brainstorming session one weekend and pronounce that you will become "the global leader of e-commerce water supplies!" How about a goal (small win) of interviewing three Web site developers within the next month to learn all you can? How about a goal of going to an educational seminar or selling *one* case of water over the Web within 90 days?

These are examples of important changes that may be vital to your survival over the next few years, but they are also small enough to be manageable and non-threatening. And, they establish a culture of change, a culture that is crucial to move you from the point of surviving, to the point of thriving.

Change Starts With You

Hopefully you're now ready to change some things in your business. If so, this might be a good time to remind you that this chapter began with a quote from Henry David Thoreau saying that, "Things Do Not Change; We Change." I hate to be the one to tell you, but for things to change within your business, *you're* going to have to change, *personally*.

A wonderful woman named Jewell Parker is a proven, successful business owner and an 8-steps workshop graduate. She previously owned a temporary employment franchise, which she successfully sold. Now, she has a business in Austin called The Meeting Place, a corporate meeting facility. When Jewell was going through the 8 steps in an eight-week format, the group challenged her to make a few small changes in her life. As a start, we asked her to go to a restaurant she had never been to before and to report back to the group the following week. A simple little comfort zone exercise.

But when we met the next week, Jewell sheepishly admitted that she had not been to a new restaurant. "I can't believe this," she said, "but every time I would start out to find a new place, I'd get in my car and it was almost as if the car had a mind of its own: It would head toward a well-known and comfortable place."

Since we were holding our meetings at The Meeting Place, I asked Jewell this: "If it's that hard for you to try something new in your life, what do you think is going on in your business, outside of this door?"

The obvious answer was: "nothing new." How can you expect your business to adapt to change, if you can't introduce change into your personal life? Thoreau was right. It took *four* weeks for Jewell to visit a new restaurant. Soon afterwards, she started changing the strategy of her business. She also started playing soccer with her daughter. And cut off her long hair! She looks great and business has never been better. All because she went to a new restaurant? Of course not. But I do believe it was, in part, because she started the object in motion, and one small change led to others. She became conscious of small wins and of how to build on them. Please don't discount the enormous power of this process before you have tried it. You will surprise yourself.

Do you take the same route to work everyday? Try a new one. How long has it been since you've worn something purple? I dare you to have your hair cut by someone new…in a new style. Treat yourself to a monthly massage. Talk to three strangers today. Park in a different spot. The more discomfort these small changes cause, the better, for that feeling of discomfort is the proof that you're stretching a comfort zone to a new dimension.

The remaining steps will all include specific business tools that will enable you to calculate the potential impact to your business model and your bottom line. You will be able to determine precisely what your business model must look like in order to support your lifetime goals. But guess what these steps will also call for? That's right—some incremental changes to the way you're doing business now.

So, if you're ready to introduce a culture of constant change into your organization, and if you recognize that for things to change, you must also change, then let's get started making more money and recapturing some of your precious time.

Photo Map Update

Many people have successfully implemented the 8 steps by tackling one step a week for eight weeks. In addition, developing one clear image for each of the eight areas of your photo map can be done weekly. In fact, in the 8-steps workshops we employ a very effective calendar system and follow-up e-mail program to generate eight weeks of reminders. Whether or not you decide to take this approach, I am going to remind you after each step to give consideration to a separate photo map area.

The first area deals with relationships. Too often, the very relationships we use as motivation to start our own businesses, suffer as a result. The time demands of our business grow disproportionately, and while we think the people around us will understand our ignoring them, we know that our customers and creditors will not. At some point, those around us will deem our apparent indifference to them as intolerable and they will make some changes. Though the truth is we are not indifferent at all, by the time a crisis comes, it is often too late to prove this point to the ones we care about.

Your challenge is to select images that convey the type of key relationships you want to foster over the next five to ten years. With some percentage of your time, you must give these every bit of your attention—at least as much as you give to your business. Whether this is committing to someone already in your life, finding someone new, or branching out to children, grandchildren, etc., let this picture encourage you to make some changes in your business—and your life—so that you will have time for what matters most.

Doing Less, Making More

Step 2

The art of being wise is the art of knowing what to overlook.

—Henry James

In the Introduction, I laid the groundwork for several important principles that will guide you throughout this book. First, while acknowledging that small businesses have an insatiable appetite for our time and money, I promised to help you to take control of both of those assets. No step is more crucial to accomplishing this goal than Step 2. Second, I mentioned that small businesses, by their very nature, have a tendency to become very complex, very quickly. It is the reduction of that complexity that will lead to the reclaiming of your time and your money and that is also central to this chapter.

Now, a question: Would you like to do less and make more? A lot more? Would you like to do less at work, leaving more time for other important areas of your life, like health, family and leisure?

Assuming your answer is yes, I'd like to begin with the story of Claudia Post, beautifully documented by Susan Greco in a story for *Inc.* magazine. The following is my synopsis, presented with *Inc.*'s permission. See if you can relate.

Claudia began her company, Diamond Courier, in 1990 as a bicycle messenger service. A relentless salesperson, Claudia worked tirelessly during the hectic startup period, surpassing $1 million in sales in only 17 months, and $3 million within three years. By then, her company employed 40 bicycle messengers and Claudia was being honored in the local community as a dynamic and successful entrepreneur. Her customers loved her, and like most small business owners, she repeatedly said "yes" to their constant requests for her to provide new and different services.

Before she knew it, in addition to the bicycle messengers, Claudia also had 50 independent drivers for truck deliveries and was in the airfreight and several other businesses. To keep all of this on track, and to handle other back office operations, Diamond's staff had grown to about 25.

One thing that perplexed Claudia was that even as revenues continued to soar, available cash moved in the opposite direction. They were doing great, but there was never enough money to pay the bills. "Cash flow? Profit before taxes? I didn't know how to figure out any of that stuff," Claudia said, wondering if she would eventually have to invest the time to learn about things such as operations and finance.

Meanwhile, in order to meet the relentless cash demands, she *knew* she needed more sales, so she hired a sales manager from a larger company. He quickly pointed out that the absence of accurate financial information was debilitating. "When I asked how we did in the previous month," he recalls, "I'd hear things like, 'Well, we either broke even…or made $6,000.'"

Though the absence of cash was threatening to strangle the business, Claudia's instincts still told her that Diamond could eventually sell its way out of trouble—especially by relying on the bicycle messenger business, the heart and soul of the company. To solve the immediate crisis, Claudia liquidated her personal assets (all the way from securities to jewelry) just to meet payroll. It continued to frustrate her that no matter how much she managed to increase sales, she had become a slave to Diamond's insatiable appetite for cash—something she did not have, and could not figure out how to get more of. She quickly ran out of personal assets.

Your Business Or Your Life?

It is one thing when business problems impact only the business; it is quite another when they physically affect the owner. One day, as Claudia sought more sales, tried to get a grip on operations and endlessly juggled payables to stay afloat, a pain ripped through her chest. She was rushed to the hospital in an ambulance. It seemed Claudia Post had been given the ultimate choice: Your business or your life!

The good news is that Claudia's attack had been one of anxiety, not of heart failure. Either way, the painful experience woke her up to the fact that she had to make some changes in her business—and her life. She had finally been convinced that her present situation was intolerable.

First, she asked for help—an often difficult admission for some entrepreneurs. She hired Al Sloman, an industry consultant who explained that his job was to help Claudia transform from a CSO (chief sales officer) to a true CEO who understood how *all parts* of the company must work together. As Sloman began to interview Claudia, he discovered several things:

1) Diamond had diversified into at least six separate businesses, any of which might have been viable on its own, but which had very different cost structures and business models. By lumping the revenues and costs of all activities together, there was no way for Claudia to know which *individual* segments were most profitable. Or, whether it was possible that some segments were not profitable at all. Relying on the gut instinct that most entrepreneurs cherish, Claudia assured Sloman that the bicycle messenger service was Diamond's cash cow;

2) Claudia assumed that the company would generate profits if it could sell goods and services at "market prices;"

3) She assumed that growing sales volume would automatically result in cost savings (economies of scale);

4) She assumed that satisfied customers would automatically become loyal customers, and;

5) She assumed that growing sales would eventually solve all problems.

From Clouds To Columns

Sloman began a process for Diamond that goes by several names. Usually, it is referred to as ABC (activity-based costing), ABM (activity-based management), or, simply, segmentation analysis. Regardless of the name, the concept is the same: Create an individual profit-center statement (a P&L) for *each* significant source of revenue.

In other words, rather than bundling all sales together, in what I envision as one big cloud, move the individual sources of revenue into columns. Go from clouds to columns.

Determining the sources of revenue from product or service lines is usually straightforward, assuming that invoices depict what was sold, even if a single customer purchases from multiple lines. But, since profit and loss statements must also include expenses, determining the revenue columns is only half the battle and the other half—expenses—is usually harder to determine.

For one thing, there are two types of expenses that we must concern ourselves with here—direct and indirect. Please don't roll your eyes at my use of accounting jargon. I'm not an accountant and I don't expect you to be. But, there are certain accounting *concepts* that a CEO must understand in order to make crucial decisions about the future.

Direct expenses are roughly synonymous with cost of goods sold—the materials and labor used exclusively to produce the products or services in question. When Diamond was examining its bicycle messenger service, for example, direct expenses would include the amount paid directly to the messengers for each delivery. Claudia estimated that this expense was about 50% of the price she charged customers.

But there are indirect costs as well—costs that may only partially relate to a specific product or service line and are thus often thought of as part of one big "overhead" expense. Somewhere back at Diamond, for example, some percentage of the dispatchers' time, the bookkeepers' time, the lighting, telephone bills, insurance, etc., existed because the bicycle messenger business existed. Yet like most costs, Diamond considered these "general" expenses to be shared by all columns of revenue.

But if an expense is necessary only because of a particular column of revenue, shouldn't we be able to accurately match that expense with the column of revenue that demands its very existence? In other words, what is crucial here, is to recognize that each dollar of revenue triggers certain expenses. Through ABC, we attempt to precisely match each dollar of revenue with the expenses it triggers so that we will know with confidence which columns of revenue are profitable and which are not. How else could a true CEO make strategic decisions about his or her future?

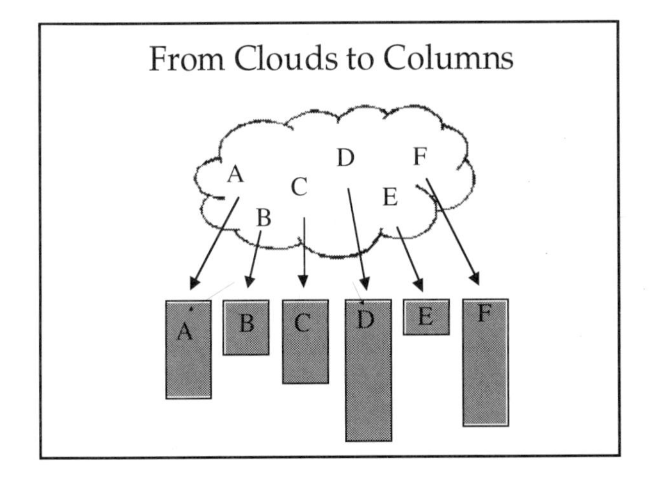

But if ABC is that important, why don't our accountants automatically do it for us? First, given the impact of resource poverty (in this case, the lack of experienced accounting expertise on staff) entrepreneurs normally hire accountants to do little more than their taxes. If they do get monthly financial statements, I'm willing to bet that the format was created by the accountant, not by the entrepreneur. Second, if accountants are left to their own devices, they will probably provide the owner with misleading information.

Please, don't misunderstand. I'm a big fan of the value of a good accountant, but ask yourself this question: How well can an accountant possibly know your business? Do they know which factors are crucial for you to measure and which are irrelevant? Do they ask questions about your customers, your competitors, your contribution margins, your retention rates, your sales efficiency, etc?

Even accountants at the major accounting firms are not likely to be experts in the crucial areas of your business. They may be experts in tax or finance or cost accounting, but few deal with what I call "strategic accounting," which is not something that's even taught in school. Strategic accounting simply means presenting the information in a manner that a business owner needs to achieve their business and personal goals. To me, that is by far the most important type of accounting (though I concede taxes still have to be paid), and yet I had to make up a name for it. Accountants are trained to create lagging indicators (how you did in the past), while CEOs should demand leading indicators (how you will do in the future). Your accountant should be familiar with ABC, but don't rush into a full implementation of such a system. I don't want you to track every penny of cost or install a complex system. I just want you to intuitively learn the value of strategic accounting—in this case, directly matching expenses to the precise source of revenue they support.

Bringing Up Baby

Back to Claudia Post. Given Sloman's experience, I can only imagine that he fought back a sardonic, if sympathetic, grin when he decided to begin his ABC analysis with Claudia's baby—the bicycle messenger business. Diamond charged customers $4.69 per bicycle delivery—the so-called market rate. Remember that Claudia assumed that if competitors were making money at that price, so too would Diamond. After all, direct costs in Claudia's mind were only 50%, leaving a good $2.35 per job as what most of us would call gross profit margin. And if that much were available to offset overhead, she *must* be making money. Right?

Wrong! Forgetting overhead for a moment, Claudia had not even correctly calculated the total *direct costs*—what was paid to the messengers. She was thinking of the obvious—their commission—but had not considered other payroll expenses including taxes and processing costs. Nor had she considered T-shirts, bonds, and other fringes. It turns out that Diamond's gross profit margin was not 50% of $4.69. Despite Claudia's "gut feel," it added up to a paltry 43 cents!

The next step was to subtract the indirect or overhead expenses that existed due to this column of revenue, and to see what the net profit contribution of the bicycle messenger service was. Here again, the true CEO must know the crucial measures of his or her business. If a CPA doesn't clearly understand the result you're seeking, for example, they might well do what *Fortune* 500 CPAs often do—that is, allocate your indirect expenses (overhead) to the various columns of revenue based on the percentage of total sales represented by each column. If Diamond had used this method, and if bicycle messengers represented 30% of sales, then 30% of total company overhead would be allocated to that "column" in order to determine overall column profitability. Do you see a problem with that?

The problem, of course, is that the real indirect cost number may be nowhere near 30%. Fortunately for Diamond,

Sloman did what you must do. To the best of his ability, he tracked down the *precise* overhead expenses that were related directly to the bicycle messenger business. He asked the dispatchers how much of their time they spent on bicycle deliveries as compared to other activities, and then, based on their fully burdened wages, assigned *that* amount to the bicycle column. He found out which telephone charges belonged to this column. He determined the percentage of rent (space), insurance and other overhead factors necessitated by this column of revenue.

Digging A Grave—*Fast*

As a result, he came up with different numbers than those that had become gospel in Claudia's entrepreneurial gut. The actual total cost of a $4.69 delivery was...are you ready? The actual cost was $9.24! The "profit" that Claudia had thought to be about 23 cents per delivery, was actually a *negative* $4.55! The company was *losing* $4.55 every time a bicycle messenger made a delivery, and yet Claudia was working herself into the hospital trying to *increase* sales volume.

With over 70,000 bicycle deliveries per year, what Claudia believed was a five-figure profit, was actually a six-figure loss. What she assumed was the lifeblood of her business, was its cancer. The information underlying these facts was the same; the only thing separating fact from fiction was the manner in which the information was presented.

So, is it good news or bad when you find out that you're sick? No one likes being sick, but at least once properly diagnosed we can begin to implement a cure. For Diamond, there was more than one illness. When properly presented (remember, the facts are the facts—it's the subjective manner of the presentation that matters), four of Diamond's six columns of revenue turned out to be money-losers. Sixty days after Sloman introduced ABC to Diamond, Claudia called her managers together and announced the obvious, if gut-wrenching, changes she had committed to.

The bicycle messenger service—her baby—was to be abandoned. Claudia feared that some of her best (or at least, largest) customers who relied on multiple services, would drop her completely. They did, but what choice did she have? She found these tough decisions—these changes—frightening, but also strangely liberating. After all, if she would give up her baby, then there would no longer be any sacred cows at Diamond. Every column of revenue would have to pull its own weight. Within two months, Diamond was also out of the airfreight and parts distribution businesses.

When the dust settled, Claudia noted that Diamond's offices were calmer and more controlled. Perhaps the adrenal startup thrill was gone but it had been replaced by a welcome and more mature demeanor. More important, it had been replaced by profits and positive cash flow, with excess cash building in the bank. By doing less, Claudia was making more. Moreover, she also had more time to herself, time, in her words, to work out daily and to laugh. She had reclaimed her business...and her life.

Some entrepreneurs may wonder what size company can best benefit from ABC. Some may wonder if they are too small to apply these principles, while others may feel they are already too sophisticated. For the small ones, I realize that the thought of abandoning *any* source of revenue is nerve-wracking. This is particularly true in the early stages when growth seems all-important. I would only remind you that, like Claudia Post, it will be far more damaging if you let unprofitable customers infiltrate your organization, than if you make sure they are paying their own way from the outset. Embracing this philosophy at the early stages may slow your initial "growth," but it will also increase your excess cash. Businesses don't fail because of a lack of growth, they fail because of a lack of cash. Keep your priorities clear at all stages of development.

Babies And Bathwater

As for those companies that might think they are too large, or too sophisticated for this approach, I would like to emphasize that the startling discoveries often provided by ABC are not reserved for small businesses. Not long ago, I attended a session at The University of Texas at Austin where the professors become students for a day. In this case, Dr. John Shank, a renowned professor from The Amos Tuck School at Dartmouth College presented us with his case study entitled "M-L Fasteners GmbH."

I'll keep it short, but the case was about a fairly large German manufacturer of snap fasteners, such as the kind you find on your jeans. ($100 million in sales with over 700 types of fasteners.) The company had an extensive cost-accounting system that had been installed by expert consultants and included 174 separate cost centers. Despite these distinctions, management philosophically grouped its products into just two broad categories—high-margin and low-margin. They were consumed with fear that the Japanese were about to flood the market and start a price war in the low-margin segment. In fact, assured by their information system that they did not have the margins to survive such an attack, management at M-L Fasteners was on the brink of abandoning the low-margin business altogether.

The problem, and the fascinating part of the case, was that the high-paid consultants, and the complicated cost-accounting system, were not allocating overhead in a manner that would aid strategic decisions. It turns out that when expenses were properly matched to columns of revenues, fasteners thought by the company to be the highest margin items were actually the lowest, and fasteners thought to be the lowest were actually the highest.

This relatively large and mature company with the sophisticated cost-accounting system was on the brink of abandoning its *most profitable* business segment due to the poor presentation of information! In my opinion this is yet another example of management sacrificing what it needs, to the accountants' description of what they can deliver. Keep in mind that accountants are responsible for the accuracy of numbers while management is responsible for the relevancy.

To help you begin developing your company's columns of revenue, I'd like to introduce a simple income statement. (Also known as a profit and loss statement.) While it is simple, it is similar to many statements produced by small businesses. Perhaps you have a software program like QuickBooks or an accountant who produces such statements for you.

Simple Income Statement

Sales (A)	$1,000,000	Total Revenue
COGS (B)	($500,000)	Direct Costs
GPM (C)	$500,000	Gross Profit Margin (A-B)
Expenses (D)	($400,000)	Rent, wages, etc.
NOI (E)	$100,000	Net Operating Income (C-D)

For now, let's just assume that these numbers are accurate and consistently prepared from period to period. (By the way, that is a *huge* assumption for most small businesses.) The result is a business model that earns 10%, pre-tax, on every dollar of sales. The result is also a business owner (assuming a sole owner) who has $100,000 available, either to pay out to themself as wages, or to reinvest (after tax) in the business in the form of retained earnings.

Playing Consultant

Let me ask you to play consultant for a moment. If an entrepreneur handed you the statement above and asked, "How am I doing?" what would you say? Think about Claudia Post for a moment, and honestly answer this question.

Here is what I have said countless times: "I have no idea how you're doing."

Why not? First, because profit is not cash. You're showing a $100,000 "profit," but for all I know you are overdrawn at the bank and incapable of meeting payroll. Secondly, with only one statement, I have no sense of direction. Is this number better or worse than last year? The year before that? By how much? Remember, it's not where you are that matters, it's which direction you are heading. And third, I only see a cloud of revenue on the top line. Within that cloud, there are probably individual columns that are contributing to the bottom line, and columns that are detracting from it. At this early stage, without an accurate matching of revenues and expenses, I just don't know. But the greater problem is, the owner probably doesn't know either.

Since every dollar of revenue triggers some related expenses, I can't begin to assess whether or not the cost structure of this business is efficient, without matching revenues to the expenses they trigger. The bottom line shown above is nothing more than a blended average of all activities, which lends no insight into where the company is making money, and where it may be losing money.

Because of an inherent inability to say "no" to customers, even the smallest business tends to evolve into a number of different activities that produce revenue. And almost immediately, most small business owners lose sight of precisely where they're making money and where they're not. Do *you* know? Worse still, like Claudia Post, their legendary "gut feel" may be 180 degrees off, leading them into a death spiral. As we were tragically reminded after the airplane crash of John Kennedy, highly intelligent people can be surrounded by perfectly accurate data, but if they don't know precisely how to interpret the data, the results can be disastrous.

If you're subtracting blended expenses from blended revenues, you can only arrive at blended profits and losses. Numbers like these conceal more than they reveal. Bad numbers are almost always worse than no numbers. Financial statements, even those prepared by CPAs, can be "accurate" yet deadly. The difference rests with your ability to understand—conceptually—what you need to know to make strategic, not accounting, decisions.

Let's consider a former client of mine who provided me with a statement similar to the one shown above. Their top line (a cloud) showed sales of about a million dollars. This number was derived from sales of hardware, packaged software they had created, and custom programming. The income statement showed costs of goods sold (COGS) of about half a million dollars, the majority of which came from direct materials such as the personal computers and peripherals they purchased and resold.

The combined gross profit margin (GPM) of $500,000 is what's available to apply toward the general overhead of the company. Whatever is left after that is deemed pre-tax profit. In this case, pre-tax profits were $100,000, and we began this discussion by trying to ascertain whether that was good or bad.

The first concern I had was not about the financial model of this company, but about the operational and managerial structures. It seemed to me that, in many ways, the business models for a hardware company, a software company and a service company, couldn't be more different. The profit margins are different, the balance sheets are unrelated...even the employees one would hire would be very different. So here was a typical small business, already suffering from resource poverty, that was trying to master not just one business model, but three! Claudia Post, as you may recall, was trying to master *six*. No matter how large or small your business may be, ask yourself how many different business models are you trying to master.

After asking some common sense questions, I was able to roughly allocate the revenue of this firm into the three major columns. Using Pareto's Law, I wasn't concerned about tracing every penny. Their revenue columns looked like this:

Hardware	Packaged Software	Custom Programming
$300,000	$500,000	$200,000

Now, wouldn't you agree that it would be a reasonable strategic question for a CEO to ask, "Which of these areas is most profitable?" Of course it would be. But if the expenses associated with each column of revenue are blended, is there any way to know? If you are paying a programmer $50,000 a year, but you have no idea what percentage of his or her time is dedicated to which columns of revenue, how do you know how much a particular column of revenue is contributing to the bottom line? You don't. You can't.

This is a vital philosophy that can make a difference of hundreds of thousands, or even millions of dollars of profit to the typical small business owner over time. Revenues trigger costs. But if you don't know *which* revenues specifically trigger *which* costs, you can't make sound strategic decisions about the future of your business. You must know this information to know where you're making money and where you're losing money. Only then can you do more of the former and less of the latter! (Some say that is the definition of consulting.)

In this case, I found that the hardware column was generating zero gross profit. In this competitive commodity marketplace, the company was essentially selling hardware at cost. But that was just the beginning of the story. As I began to ask questions about how people in the organization spent their time, I found that several spent part of their time on supporting hardware customers. As I looked around (using common sense), I saw that a disproportionate amount of space was allocated to receiving and holding inventory and spare parts — functions dedicated to the hardware column of revenue.

Think of this exercise as simply creating a P&L statement for each column of revenue. At first, give no thought to whether expenses can be subdivided in the real world. In other words, if "Joan" spends a third of her time on hardware support, put a third of Joan in that column. Don't worry right now about whether you can cut Joan into thirds!

When the common sense questions were answered in this case, I had identified $150,000 of indirect expenses that would *not* have been needed without the hardware sales. You don't have to get a calculator or spreadsheet out to assess this one, do you? What was happening in the hardware column? With gross profit margins of zero before expenses, and expenses of $150,000, they were *losing* $150,000 a year.

Reducing Sales to Increase Profits

When I say less is more, I mean that even the smallest business can often *increase* net income by *reducing* unprofitable sales. In this case, getting out of the hardware business would *reduce* sales by 30%, yet *increase* net income by 150%! Given that we can't cut Joan into thirds, we may not be able to realize all of these savings, but a 100% increase in net income is very realistic in this case. And the beauty of reduced expenses is not only that they make their way directly to the bottom line, but that they get there almost immediately. And, as with Diamond Courier, eliminating unprofitable columns of revenue also leaves us with a simpler business model to manage. It leaves us with more time to devote to other columns and other things—things important enough to you to be placed on your photo map.

Now, if one column of revenue is losing far more money than management could imagine, is it possible that another column is earning far more? It's not only possible, it's a mathematical certainty. Once we had discovered what to do less of, it was far easier to determine what to do more of. When I examined the custom programming segment (revenues of $200,000), I discovered that someone, probably an accountant, had suggested they show contract labor as a direct cost (COGS), but keep full-time personnel on the expense line as part of overhead. This left the custom programming segment with an apparent gross profit margin of $100,000 dollars, even though this ignored costs that existed only because the custom programming segment existed. Does that make sense?

For example, what about the full-time programmers? And what about personnel involved in the training and support of custom installations? What about the time it took for full-time programmers to oversee the contract labor? What about an accurate estimate of the space (and rent) used by this group, and what about the expense of computers and other dedicated equipment?

When these additional directly related expenses were captured, they approximated $150,000 dollars. Which meant that the Custom Software business, if viewed as a stand-alone profit center, did *not* have a positive contribution margin of $100,000, but rather it had a *negative* contribution margin of $50,000 dollars a year.

If this were your company, would the information we've uncovered so far make you excited to get to the packaged software segment? It excited me! There, we found that the $500,000 column of revenue triggered COGS of only about $100,000. Why? Because obviously the cost to duplicate a software package, which includes not much more than a cardboard box and a CD, is not very great. The contribution margin of the packaged software business (a radically different model than either the hardware or custom programming business) was $400,000 dollars. The share of overhead directly attributable to this column of revenue was only about $100,000 dollars—mostly for a share of the rent, some storage space and one dedicated programmer who handled technical support and annual upgrades.

The final conclusion? The company was showing a blended profit of $100,000 because (unknown to them) they were *losing* $200,000 in two parts of their business, and making $300,000 in another. When I first introduced the income statement shown above, I asked the question of whether or not the $100,000 bottom line was "good." How would you answer that question now?

Income Statement by Product Line

	Hardware	Pkg. Software	Programming	Total
Sales	$300,000	$500,000	$200,000	$1,000,000
COGS	(300,000)	(100,000)	(100,000)	(500,000)
GPM	$0	$400,000	$100,000	$500,000
Expenses	(150,000)	(100,000)	(150,000)	(400,000)
NOI	($150,000)	$300,000	($50,000)	$100,000

The same information that portrayed a profit of $100,000 for the company, now shows that there are actually two losers and one big winner among the product lines. This information is crucial to making strategic choices and knowing where to invest your time and money.

Get Over It

Do you think that changing the manner in which this information was presented changed management's priorities? Their strategic focus? Do you think that they now knew what to do more of and what to do less of? Like fast cars and big diamonds, there is an ego association with large sales numbers. There is a natural tendency for entrepreneurs to seek to increase their *top line* at all costs. ("Oh yeah, we did $3 million last year.") That top line is almost always the way we describe our firms. But, while it may be true that a part of our ego hesitates to lop sales off the top line, when the amount of money (and excess cash) in your pocket could potentially triple, I suggest you just get over it.

Is it really that simple? Well, it can be, but of course there can also be potential complications in the implementation. It is possible that some business segments (columns of revenue) are linked strategically to others. For example, what if the hardware customers above (who created a negative profit) were also the packaged software customers, and would not buy one without the other? Then, we would have to combine those two columns and make decisions accordingly. Start thinking about how to apply this process to your business. Here's how it worked for a few others:

• When Jewell Parker did this analysis after an 8-steps workshop, she found the primary columns of revenue from The Meeting Place were room rental, equipment rental and catering. When she identified which expenses were triggered by which columns of revenue, she realized where her profits were coming from (it was not where she had thought), and radically changed the nature of her pricing and marketing strategies.

• When "Bill" did this analysis during an 8-steps workshop, he discovered, to his surprise, that the sale of used computers was *not* his most profitable column of revenue—rather, it was barely breaking even.

• When Rob Cullen, president of Ace Fire Equipment, Co., did this analysis after an 8-steps workshop, he was able to divest a column of revenue that not only was unprofitable, but was a frustrating and distasteful part of his business. His profits and his employees' morale went up immediately.

• When Pat Flanary, president of Advantage Mortgage Network, Inc., did this analysis during an 8-steps workshop, she discovered that her margins were highest on a mortgage product that offered the lowest commission to her salespeople. She corrected that, and soon thereafter celebrated a dramatic increase in profits.

Once you have analyzed your columns of revenue, it is fairly straightforward to allocate fewer, if any, resources on the losers and more on the winners. Like Claudia Post, you must be willing to abandon activities that do not fall into one of your *profitable* columns of revenue. Spend your efforts building the profitable columns higher, rather than adding more columns in haphazard fashion. Whenever possible, grow up, not out. Master one business model before adding new ones.

Photo Map Update

The next area of development for your photo map is that of intellectual challenge. Resource poverty and the demands on your time can squeeze out time for new intellectual pursuits. Using your brain may be required to build a Web site or learn a new contact management system, but there is great value in learning *outside* of your primary field of interest. Einstein and many other geniuses believed that their greatest breakthroughs came when enjoying activities completely unrelated to their specialties. With each new study on aging, we also learn that challenging our minds is what keeps them sharp well into our later years.

Find intellectually challenging pursuits that you want to have mastered in 5-10 years, and depict those with a photo map image. Some examples of these are learning chess, learning to play the piano or speak a foreign language, reading, writing, teaching, traveling and going to educational seminars. By the way, the number of courses you can take online today is growing by the hour.

Discovering Ideal Customers

Step 3

Divide et impera.
(Divide and Rule.)

—**Niccoló Machiavelli**

Imagine your ideal customer. This is the customer who is increasing the level of business they give to you each year, the customer who is intensely loyal, who works with you to solve problems, and who doesn't seem to mind paying relatively high prices.

Can there really be such a customer—an Ideal Customer (IC)?

Not only can there be, but there *must* be for your business to succeed, and most businesses already have one or more ICs. The problem is, following the same logic as in Step 2, many entrepreneurs may not know which of their customers are ideal and which are not. Worse still, relying on their proverbial gut feel, their hunches may be precisely wrong.

Discovering which customers are ideal begins by examining your existing customer base. Like sifting through silt in hopes of finding a gold nugget, you must sift through your entire customer base in hopes of finding a precious few ICs. Naturally, the other part of this process is the commitment to free yourself of the burdens imposed by less-than-ideal customers. Once again, less becomes more.

Does this mean that after admonishing you to narrow your product/service focus in Step 2, that I am now asking you to narrow your customer base as well? Am I asking you to potentially shed even more sources of revenue?

Yes, but only in the short term. Despite my admonitions to "do less," I'm well aware that some readers will insist that they need *more* customers, not fewer. And they may be right. We'll get to that, but for now, I ask for your patience. Like most skills, from gardening to house painting to selling, it is the preparation phase that is the most time-consuming and the most critical. We speak of planting a new flowerbed, but it is getting the bed ready to plant that comes first and that takes the most time. Unless the weeds have been meticulously pulled, and the soil tilled and fertilized, we are risking certain doom for our beautiful new plants and the loss of our entire investment of time and money. Painting kitchen cabinets can be rewarding and even fun—but only if the cabinets have already been sanded, the hardware removed, and the remainder of the kitchen carefully masked. All of which is painstakingly hard work.

Getting new customers can also be easy, if you don't mind getting the *wrong* customers. But, since that will make your life miserable down the road, I feel strongly that it's worth the time and preparation to get *ideal* customers from the outset—or at least to know them when you see them.

For those hell-bent on building the largest possible company, rest assured that the last few steps of this book will help you to grow your business to virtually any dimension that you desire, including higher levels of sales, profitability and cash flow. But first, we've got to tend to a little weeding, tilling, sanding and preparing. So get your work clothes on and let's get started.

I hope that Step 2 proved that most businesses, by lumping all of their sources of revenue together, effectively lose sight of the degree to which individual products and services are genuinely profitable, if profitable at all. But even after these clouds of revenue are properly reconstructed as columns, the columns will still contain individual customers who are profitable and customers who are not.

Just as with product/service lines, if you are lumping all of your customers into a single cloud and producing a single profit and loss statement, it becomes impossible to tell the customers who are winners from those who are losers. How can you begin to make vital strategic decisions about asset allocation (especially your time), when it is not known which customers are generating profits and which are producing losses? As you contemplate this, please bear in mind that, like Claudia Post, it is entirely possible that your "gut feel" in this area is 180 degrees wrong.

Be Selective

Having too many of the wrong customers causes problems that go far beyond the obvious financial implications. Negative customers adversely affect employee morale and demand so much of your time that the opportunity costs of serving them ensures that your ideal customers will get less than your best. In struggling to keep the wrong customers, you invariably jeopardize the right ones. In trying to be all things to all people, you excel at serving none. Just as life is too short to have a business that does not support your desired lifestyle, life is too short for contentious customer relationships. The small firm simply doesn't have the emotional capacity to deal with constant negativism. Sales at any cost almost always cost too much.

You have the ability to *select* ideal customers for your business, but first, you must carefully define exactly what an IC is. ICs often share the following traits, and one of your most important goals should be to focus *all* of the resources of your firm on attracting and retaining only those customers who:

- provide (or will eventually provide) the highest levels of profitability;
- are most likely to grow significantly over time (grow up, not out);
- are least likely to leave;
- will be most interested in your *new* products and services;
- are the most fun and enjoyable to work with;
- require the least effort to obtain the highest profits.

The search for ICs begins within your existing customer base, but it is important to begin the search with a particular mindset. First, in order to ascertain the profitability of individual customers, you must start with a mindset that recognizes that all customers are different and, therefore, must be treated differently. Still, given the limited resources of a small business, there should at least be *similarities* among your most important customer groups. Perhaps they are all of a similar size, or from a single industry group. Perhaps they share a common geography or are all government entities. Being conscious of these similarities will help you to develop a focused strategy that will invariably lead to greater profits and a more efficient (and enjoyable) business model.

The Same But Different?

Did I just say that your customers should be the same but different? Yes. Think of customers as you would think of your children. They will share certain characteristics (they will "look" somewhat alike) but each will have different personalities, and, within the narrow range of products and services you offer, each will need to be respected for their individual "personality" traits. Just as children go through different stages of growth, from infants, to toddlers, to adolescents, so, too, do your customers go through different stages of growth. Just as you wouldn't discipline an infant for spilling milk, or place your teenager in a highchair, you must learn to treat your ideal customers in a manner appropriate to their stage of development.

While trendy gurus have been known to say that customers are for life, they most certainly are not. Since customers expect and demand different levels of service at different stages, to deny that customers go through cycles will preclude you from ever servicing them to your best ability, and therefore, preclude you from ever earning a fair financial return on that customer. To determine the stage of development of an individual customer, you must segment customers in a way that reveals their differences...and similarities.

One of the best approaches for segmenting your customers, so that you can determine which you want to keep and which you can't afford to keep, is to use a matrix. In the following pages, I will introduce you to three matrices, each with particular strengths. When used together, they will provide valuable insights that can reshape your firm's strategy in a very short period of time.

The first and simplest matrix was detailed in another excellent case study prepared by *Inc.* magazine. The company involved was CRI—Custom Research Inc., a 14-year-old marketing research firm. The problem facing CRI was that despite the rapid increase in its customer base to 157 customers, its sales and profits had stalled. In hopes of learning which customers exhibited the most ideal personality traits, CRI decided to place their existing customers into one of four quadrants. Please take a moment to study these four categories and ask yourself what they mean.

High Volume Low Margin Q2	Q1 High Volume High Margin
Low Volume Low Margin Q3	Q4 Low Volume High Margin

Volume / Margin Matrix

Since most small businesses suffer from a shortage of skilled workers and available time, Q2 (high volume/low margin) and Q3 (low volume/low margin) would typically be the *worst* places to have a lot of customers. By definition, just *having* a customer triggers substantial overhead expenses, administrative support and the potential for problems. For small businesses, the mere overhead burden associated with any customer, dictates that profit margins on those customers cannot be at the low end of the scale. In other words, don't try to compete with Wal-Mart. While a small business may survive on narrow profit margins, they need flush profit margins in order to thrive. The 8 steps in this book are all designed to considerably fatten profit margins.

Without knowing the inner thoughts of CRI's management, we can reasonably assume that for them, the right side of this matrix (the high margin side) was the "good half," and the left side (the low margin side) was the "bad half." Yet when CRI plotted their customers, here is what they found. (The number of customers in each quadrant is indicated by the numbers in parentheses.)

High Volume Low Margin (11)	High Volume High Margin (10)
Low Volume Low Margin (101)	Low Volume High Margin (33)

Volume / Margin Matrix

Do you detect a problem?

The Power Of Saying No

During a period of rapid growth, CRI had been unable to say "no!" to virtually any new customer or customer demand. No doubt prizing sales over profits, they were unaware that the bulk of their resources (financial and human) had been tied up in servicing more than a hundred borderline and money-losing accounts. As with Claudia Post, a different presentation of the same facts stunned CRI management and dictated a change. They realized they could no longer try to be all things to all people. To do so would spread them too thin, ensuring poor service for even their very best customers, dramatically increasing the chances that those ideal customers would leave.

What would you do in this case? If you said you would get rid of the low margin, non-producing customers, you are right. CRI "fired" their weak customers. *Inc.* magazine described it this way: "In effect, the company's new *growth* strategy was to turn away revenues—revenues it had come to count on."

Is this starting to sound familiar? Did somebody say something about less being more? I realize that it is almost sacrilegious for entrepreneurs to willingly give up a customer. But think of the resources that CRI freed up once this unpleasant, but necessary task was done—resources that could now be focused on their ideal, high-margin customers. And think of the changes in morale when some 40 customers who were taking up time, but not contributing to the firm's health, were dismissed. Remember, the surest way to build the profitability of your firm is to build your relatively few columns of revenue higher, not to add more columns. (Grow up, not out.) Only after taking this bold action, was CRI able to focus on that effort.

And it paid off. In fact, growing up and not out has magical mathematical effects. CRI's executives calculated that, despite ultimately firing a whopping 67% of their total customer base, they needed to increase sales by only 20% to their remaining customers to reclaim their previous level of total sales! And, they would arrive at that level of sales with substantially higher margins, higher profits, greater customer satisfaction and much higher employee morale than before. Is it time for you to prune your customer base?

Another huge benefit for CRI was that once the characteristics of an "Ideal Customer" were uncovered, they could then be applied to prospective customers as well. What characteristics did their ideal customers share? Were they public or private? For profit or not for profit? Headquarters or branches? This is information that came out of the screening process. As CRI sifted through the silt and became aware of what was working today, they simultaneously became aware of what would work even better tomorrow. They reduced their chances of repeating earlier mistakes by adopting a strict definition of their Ideal Customer. They learned to say "no," even to the extent of hiring a "gatekeeper" whose job it is to ensure that all prospects meet the profile of an Ideal Customer. They learned to say "yes" to customers who had real sales potential, and to focus their scarce and valuable resources on only those customers.

While the CRI matrix represents an important first-level screen that any company can quickly apply and learn from, it does not screen for everything. By focusing exclusively on sales and gross profit margins, we still lack some vital information. You may recall from Step 2 how the failure to understand and properly match *indirect* costs caused managers of large and small companies to nearly make fatal mistakes. Claudia Post had a "feel" for sales and margins, yet completely misunderstood the negative bottom line impact of her bicycle messenger business. The managers at M-L Fasteners had detailed information on sales and gross profit margins, yet almost abandoned the wrong product line. To make certain that you don't make these same mistakes, you must utilize a second customer matrix that focuses on how much it costs to serve a particular type of customer.

Keep in mind that some customers, even those who are equal in size, cost more to serve than others. Some are extremely demanding, while some are quite cooperative. Some are strict and sticklers for detail, while others have the big-picture mentality. Some have the personality of scratching and clawing for every penny, while others seem to never mention price. Some seem to relish contentious relationships while others seek more harmony. The result is that two of your Ideal Customers could order exactly the same goods and services from you, yet based on *their* personalities (not yours) one of them would be far more profitable to you than the other. At the extreme, one of them might not even be worth retaining as a customer! This is what I mean when I say that even similar customers will display different personalities and must, therefore, be treated differently.

The Harvard Model

Obviously, the gap between the gross profit margin from a specific customer (as reflected in the first matrix), and the total cost to serve that same customer (as reflected in the second matrix), is getting awfully close to something we could call profit. Calculating the total cost to serve each customer, then, is vital in order to determine the profitability of that individual customer. Assuming that the typical small business will not have (and probably doesn't need) a detailed cost-accounting system that can track and allocate every dollar of overhead for specific customers, this second matrix can help. This one comes from a *Harvard Business Review* article appropriately entitled *Manage Customers for Profits (Not Just Sales).* This article may be a bit more detailed than most business owners care for, but it makes the same crucial points as the *Inc.* article, that is, even large and sophisticated companies often do not know which of their individual customers are profitable and which are not. And, more to the point, that they will often be surprised when they discover the truth.

You will use the Harvard model to segment your existing customers by both the prices they are willing to pay (their price sensitivity) and the total costs to serve them—both results of *their* unique personalities. Notice the titles given to each quadrant. I think they are self-explanatory, but useful. Carriage Trade can be likened to a luxury car buyer. They will pay for the Mercedes or Lexus, but they will demand immediate roadside assistance, loaner cars, car washes, etc. Private clubs, personal services such as landscaping and five-star hotels are other examples of Carriage Trade practitioners.

Passive customers may buy the same products and services as those in the Carriage Trade quadrant, but are not as demanding of what they receive in return. Or, they may buy because they are brand conscious, such as those who pay a premium for Tylenol, even though they know it is chemically identical to the generic acetaminophen. Upscale retail buyers of products by Ralph Lauren, Rolex and Nike might fall into the Passive quadrant.

Bargain Basement customers don't demand much of their suppliers, but the trade-off is that they *insist* on rock-bottom prices. Examples of these might include shoppers at huge "depot" stores who gladly accept having to help themselves as they walk bare floors through crowded aisles, before getting to long checkout lines.

Aggressive customers want it all. They aggressively negotiate lower pricing while simultaneously negotiating higher deliverables, increasing your cost to serve them. You don't have to be a CPA to appreciate that lower prices and higher costs to serve will not get you where you want to go.

Into which quadrant do most of your customers fall? Can you instinctively make distinctions between them? And then ask yourself where your Ideal Customers *should* be?

Passive High Prices Low Cost to Serve	**Carriage Trade** High Prices High Cost to Serve
Bargain Basement Low Prices Low Cost to Serve	**Aggressive** Low Prices High Cost to Serve

The Harvard Model

As with the CRI matrix, you can quickly and easily screen 100% of your customers using the Harvard model. The exception might be if you have *thousands* of customers, in which case it would be helpful to find common characteristics (order size, order frequency, products ordered, etc.) and lump them together into a manageable number of customer "types."

Once you have placed your customers, or customer types, into the proper quadrant, you can again invoke our friend Pareto and pay attention primarily to your largest customers. Rather than using dots as before, consider using circles to represent your customers—the larger the circle, the larger the annual revenue from that customer. This is an ideal way to get a feel for the relative importance of each, and is especially important with this matrix since it does not otherwise reveal sales volume.

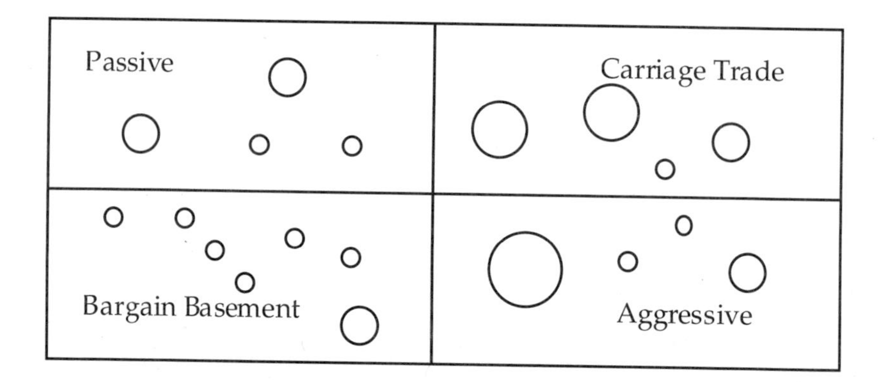

Which Customers Should Go?

Given the nature of small businesses, most managers will find that their best customers (not to be confused with their most prevalent customers) fall into two quadrants. Can you guess which two? This time, instead of the two quadrants on the right side, most small businesses will find their best customers in the two quadrants across the top—the two quadrants where customers are willing to pay high prices regardless of the total cost to serve. Once again, healthy profit margins become the obvious key to moving from a position of surviving to one of thriving.

Once you have completed this exercise, you should again spend time trying to find commonality among your best customers. To the extent that you can identify shared characteristics, or personality traits, you are moving forward in defining your Ideal Customer and will have traveled light years toward a focused and profitable strategy of effective customer prospecting, attainment and retention. Your profitable columns will soon begin growing faster than you could have imagined, reaching for the sky…or at least for the images on your photo map.

Like medical tests, the weakness of these matrix tools is that while they can screen for certain things, one tool by itself cannot screen for everything. That's why, like your physician, you'll use a combination of tools. While you will uncover many valuable insights by quickly placing your customers in *both* of the matrices described above, you are still left with one glaring weakness. Test your management skills and think for a moment what that weakness might be. Can you determine what it is? (Hint: I have already mentioned in this book that it doesn't matter where you are, only which direction you are heading.) I think this third and final matrix will help explain.

A Dog Is A Dog

Many years ago, the prestigious Boston Consulting Group (BCG) designed a matrix to help *Fortune* 500 companies manage their investments in various business units and subsidiaries. The tool became a classic, coining such terms as "cash cow" in the process. The value of the matrix (technically called the Growth Share Portfolio Matrix) was that it highlighted the fact that these business units went through lifecycles, and that each stage of the lifecycle had different financial characteristics—especially those relating to growth and cash flow. For example, an early-stage or start-up business would require investment, and would not be expected to generate a return on that investment for some period of time. In the early stages it would, by definition, be a net user of cash. This seems logical, doesn't it? Thus, a negative cash flow in the early stages was not considered troublesome. It was expected. It was simply budgeted for and tracked.

This same business unit, however, at some point in the future, would be expected to turn profitable and to then produce a positive cash flow. (A return on investment or, ROI.) The type of business (personality) would determine exactly how long this turnaround should take and the magnitude of the overall return. Some units would take longer than others, and some would generate higher or lower returns.

Do you see what's radically different about the BCG matrix? Notice that the characteristic of *movement* (or growth) from quadrant to quadrant has now been introduced. Recognizing that business units do not just stand still is the real genius behind this deceptively powerful tool. In recognizing that, BCG realized that individual performance, measured at a given point in time, would never give a true indication of the *total* return over the *life* of the investment. A calculation of ROI made at a point in time (while in one particular quadrant) would always yield a misleading conclusion—too low in the early phases and too high in the latter phases. And these misleading conclusions would encourage managers to make bad decisions, or discourage them from making good ones.

It struck me during my early days of consulting with small businesses that while few have separate business units, all have unique entities that require investment, generate revenues, move through lifecycles and that should be measured individually. Can you think of what these unique entities are called?

I hope you said *customers!* The more I began to work with the BCG matrix, the more obvious it became to me that there was little difference between a business unit for a big company and an Ideal Customer for a small firm. Your Ideal Customers are your "subsidiaries," and, just like a giant company, you must constantly assess and adjust your level of investment in, and your return on, each. You must have tools that can help you make the difficult decision of when to shift investments from one to another and of where to allocate your assets, including your most important asset—time.

Just as business units go through cycles, including phases of investments and phases of returns, so too, will your Ideal Customers. In order to take the appropriate actions at the appropriate times (including strategic matters such as investment, service, pricing, etc.), it becomes imperative for you to know not only which phase your ideal customers are in, but which direction they are heading.

The two variables that you have at your disposal for creating a positive return over the life of a customer are investment and disinvestment. For most small businesses, which tend to be weighted toward services, this usually means simply providing more service, or less service. Knowing when to provide more and when to provide less, despite the short-term impact on cash flow, will dramatically affect your *overall* profitability, yet can only be intelligently determined by tracking your customer's "flow" through the different stages of the lifecycle.

When placing a key customer into a quadrant of the BCG matrix, you automatically answer not only the question of where the customer is presently, but also the more important question of which direction they are heading. Let's look at the BCG matrix, and as we do, let me leave the *Fortune* 500 world behind and focus on the utility of this tool for the small business owner. First, notice that I have added a box to the right of the matrix labeled "prospects." I hope that you have already vowed to be more rigorous and disciplined in your search for Ideal Customers—beginning in the prospecting phase. I hope that, knowing the pain that getting the wrong customers will ultimately cause, you will not try to be all things to all people. And I hope, therefore, that all of the prospects in your prospect pool will share the personality traits identified during your Ideal Customer screens using the previous two matrices.

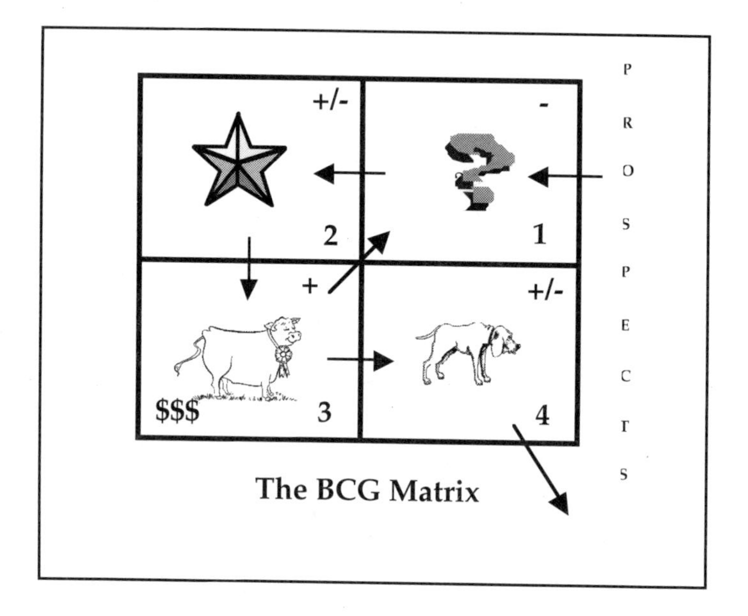

The BCG Matrix

When prospects first become customers, they are placed in the Question Mark quadrant. This simply acknowledges that, even though they meet your strict criteria as a *potential* Ideal Customer, one never knows for certain whether or not the relationship will blossom. There are many variables on both sides of the equation. For example, the purchasing manager that you spent a year winning over could take maternity leave the next day, or accept that new position...in Zimbabwe!

When Negative Cash Flow Is A Good Thing

Also note that during the Question Mark phase, your firm's cash flow is expected to be negative. The assumption is that when a customer is new, there will be an investment required on your part. This investment may be large and tangible (such as the purchase of specialized equipment), or small and intangible (such as retraining your employees to adhere to new procedures), but expenses will be incurred...investments will be made.

It is also important to note that this outflow of cash (investment) usually begins *before* the customer is actually a customer. Costs incurred *prior to* the sale must also be considered as part of the *total cost* to serve a given customer. Many sales involve long and complex pre-sale activities such as sales calls, travel, entertainment, presentation materials, proposals and prototypes. All too frequently, these costs and others (such as the investment of time of top management) are not allocated to the specific customers who trigger them. If they are not, how could you ever calculate an accurate return on your total investment in that customer?

As your new customers (Question Marks) become integrated into your organization (what Step 4 calls "growing roots"), and, as their sales volume starts to increase, they will ideally move into the Star quadrant. In this quadrant, cash flow may either remain negative or turn positive, depending on the *rate* of your customer's growth. Remember, rapid growth eats cash. If a customer is growing rapidly, the "costs to serve" (your investment) that led to a negative cash flow in the Question Mark quadrant, will continue to grow in advance of profits. Even though the word "star" sounds wonderful, and this quadrant is highly desirable, so long as the customer is growing rapidly, you will normally find your investment continues to exceed your return, resulting in a continuing negative cash flow. Planning for how you will cover this shortfall is essential to surviving long enough to thrive.

So how long is that? When does the positive cash flow commence? At some point in time, the *rate of growth* of your ideal customer will start to slow. This may be months or years after the initial sale, depending on your business model and industry. Please notice that I did not say that sales would necessarily decline in absolute terms, but rather that the *rate of growth* of sales must eventually slow. As the rate of growth of a customer slows, so will your investment—your cost to serve. It may no longer be necessary, for example, to buy new equipment. What you have previously acquired may even be paid for by now. It may no longer be necessary for you to hire new people, or learn new procedures. You will already have what you need to service this account—in fact, you may be able to *reduce* your deployment of resources in absolute terms, without damaging the customer relationship. For example, you may be so far up the learning curve at this point that customer service questions become predictable, and perhaps can be handled by one representative instead of two. Your total cost to serve this particular customer starts to decline.

Can you predict the almost immediate result? Since every dollar of expense reduction goes straight to the bottom line, you will suddenly find yourself in a period of excessive profitability and cash flow, which the BCG matrix rightfully refers to as the Cash Cow. Isn't it interesting that the most highly desirable cash flow in a customer's lifecycle comes *after* their heyday of rapidly increasing sales?

In the preceding paragraph, I referred to "excessive profitability and cash flow." I used this phrase intentionally, in hopes of raising an eyebrow or two. Are "excessive" profits sinful? Many entrepreneurs I've worked with seem to think so. They actually become uncomfortable when they find themselves in a position of extracting what *seems like* "excessive profits" from a valuable, long-time customer. They think of excessive profits in negative terms such as gouging or soaking. (Or, in deference to our matrix, milking.) They are forever talking about reducing prices to give this customer a fair shake, or perhaps to rekindle their previous levels of growth.

ROC Rocks

But they need to change their thinking and the BCG matrix can help them to do just that. At the very core of the BCG matrix is the ability to conceptualize that it is *not* the profitability at a given point in time that matters, but the profitability over the *lifetime* of the customer, or, what I call "return on customer" (ROC). Failure to view customer profitability over the projected life of the customer will almost guarantee that you price too high during early stages (thus discouraging customers from expanding their business with you), and price too low during the later stages, thus giving up profits that you have fairly earned

There is also profit to be squeezed from the final quadrant, erroneously entitled "Dog." In the first two quadrants, you have invested, invested and invested some more. You have taken the entrepreneurial risk of a planned negative cash flow. You did this, consciously or otherwise, because you anticipated a return on that investment sufficient to make your risk worthwhile. That return is paid off in Quadrant III (and to a lesser extent in Quadrant IV) and you must resist the temptation to give back to your customer the fair return that you have earned. Quadrant IV simply describes a customer with declining sales, not just in rate of growth, but also in nominal terms. Assuming this customer cannot be miraculously returned to the Question Mark quadrant (to start the life cycle anew), it is essential that you *not* allow yourself to return to a negative cash flow position with this customer. In fact, you must be aggressive in *reducing* your cost to serve in advance of the declining sales, thus maintaining a marginally positive cash flow position until the end.

This can be emotionally difficult, because, by definition, this customer was once an Ideal Customer. As you reduce service and forego additional investment, the customer may complain, or even threaten to leave you. But hey, they're leaving you anyway whether they know it or not. When it's over, it's over, and when negative cash flow again looks imminent after a long-term relationship, it's time to say, "Thanks for your business...may we help you find a new supplier for your remaining work?" Then, re-deploy your assets (human and financial) on Question Marks and Stars, letting the evolution of your "ideal" customer base continue.

What's It Worth?

These three powerful screening tools have shown you how to glean ideal customers from your customer base and to create a profile for future customers based on sales volume, gross profit margin, price sensitivity, total cost to serve, and the rate and direction of growth. That can take you a long way to filling your company with Ideal Customers, but there is still one important personality trait that none of these matrices has helped us to identify, but which is critical to customer selection—the lifetime value of an Ideal Customer.

Let me ask you this vitally important question: From start to finish, from Question Mark to Dog, from first nickel invested to last nickel earned…how much is your Ideal Customer worth to you?

This is a number worth knowing. Figure out this number—the lifetime value of a customer (LV/C)—and you will be well on your way to figuring out exactly what you need to do in business to get everything you want out of life! There will be much more on this in Step 4.

Too many small businesses, in a desperate grab for sales at all costs, go into customer relationships with their heads in the sand. They say to themselves, "We'll invest whatever it takes to *get* this customer…and pray that we will eventually, miraculously, figure out a way to make money on them." (Do I hear some dot-com company executives saying, "But isn't that how it's supposed to work?")

Like any set of projections, the process involved in determining LV/C is as important as the result. The process forces you to ask many important questions about the viability of your customers and, therefore, of your business model. It forces you to look at your own goals and commitments, as well as the personalities of your Ideal Customers. To help you understand the importance of determining this number, let me ask you this question: How much would you be willing to pay for $100,000 to be received over the next five years? Would you pay $50,000? $95,000? $100,000? $125,000?

The answer to this question depends on several things, including the timing of the receipt of the $100,000. That is, will it be received as a lump sum, in equal installments, or perhaps in unequal installments? And what is your confidence level that the money will in fact be received at all? Is it guaranteed? By whom? Once these issues have been factored in, you should be able to state what you would be willing to pay for this income stream.

Now, change the word "pay" in the previous sentence to "invest" and you have determined how much you should be willing to invest in an Ideal Customer whose lifetime value to you is $100,000. Simply stated, if you know over their lifetime what a customer is worth, you know what level of early investment is warranted on your part. If Taco Bell thought you were going to come into their stores only once and order a 99 cent burrito, they could not afford to invest in such clean stores and well-trained employees. But they don't see their Ideal Customer as worth 99 cents. No, they've calculated their Ideal Customer as worth $12,000 over their lifetime! Do you see how that casts a completely different light on how Taco Bell invests its money and how it treats its customers—even on those occasions when they do come in just to spend 99 cents?

Or consider the example of a printer who has obtained a new customer expected to produce $100,000 a year in sales with gross margins of 30%, or $30,000 per year. And, suppose that in order to service that customer, the printer must purchase a new $45,000 piece of equipment, which is to be dedicated to the new customer. It's obvious, isn't it, that the printer can't recover the entire cost of the equipment in the first month, or even in the first year? Does this mean that the prudent business decision would be to decline this customer? This question is almost impossible to answer if the LV/C is unknown. If the LV/C is known, however, there should be little hesitation in sustaining a period of negative cash flow, knowing that the difference will be more than made up in subsequent years.

You will also find that knowing the LV/C is one of the most effective ways to forecast sales and develop a specific plan to meet all of your business and personal financial goals. Rather than thinking of increasing sales in dollar terms, it can be more empowering to think in terms of the specific number of customers that need to be added.

Perhaps the most troublesome aspect of the LV/C approach to Ideal Customer selection and management, is the concern over what happens if a customer leaves *after* your initial investment, but *before* you have had an opportunity to capture a fair return? For example, what if the print customer above goes to a competitor after the machine had been purchased on their behalf, but before they had placed orders for the second year?

Well, as the song says: don't worry, be happy. They *can't* leave you...and Step 4 will explain why not.

Photo Map Update

The photo map image for Step 3 is that of Contribution. Based on the truism that it is better to give than receive, this represents that magical feeling of self-worth that makes the bad times better and the good times great. Whether you dedicate just one lunch a month for reading to kids, or devote a percentage of your profits to save the world, a feeling of contribution makes the desire to succeed in business bigger and greater than just ourselves. When you go all out to make more by doing less, there will be both more time and more money for others as well. As an example, at times, I have used young runners on a track as my symbol of contribution, reminding me to give my money and my time to programs that encourage underprivileged youths to participate in athletic activities.

Growing Roots

Step 4

Because they had no root,
they withered away.

—St. Matthew

I hope that by now you can see how concentrating your efforts on Ideal Customers is going to make work more enjoyable and life, simpler. Or is it the other way around? Not only will you be saner and happier, but so will your best customers and everyone knows that happy customers are loyal customers. Right? *Wrong!*

A Harvard Business Review study revealed the shocking truth that 65% to 85% of customers who defect classified themselves as either satisfied or very satisfied at the time of their defection. They were happy, yet they left. I get such a strong reaction to this statement during my workshops that I want to make it again, with a twist: Loyal customers are always satisfied, but satisfied customers are not always loyal. In other words, despite all the hype we hear about caring for the customer, customer satisfaction does *not* necessarily correlate to customer *retention*, and it is customer retention that impacts the bottom line. It is customer retention that is essential to the health of your business, and it is customer retention that you really want to build when you speak of building loyalty.

How important is customer retention? Most business owners have heard statistics citing that it is seven to ten times more costly to acquire a new customer than to retain an existing one. While this may be true, retention becomes of even greater importance when the focus is placed, not on customer acquisition costs, but on *profits*—profits over the lifetime of the customer. In this crucial measure, a separate Harvard article calculated that a mere 5% *decrease* in customer defections can *increase* profits by 25% to 85%. Now that's leverage! And that proves why your time and attention—your scarce resources—must be spent on retaining customers. (This assumes, of course, that you have already culled your customer base to Ideal Customers only.)

But, if customer satisfaction does not lead to customer retention, then what does? Goodness knows, as entrepreneurs, we've been bombarded with books and articles and seminars touting the importance of offering great, personalized service. But if good service alone is not enough, how do we retain ICs long enough to earn a fair return? How do we prevent them from leaving us just as they are entering the positive cash flow quadrants?

Follow The Money

The answer to these questions is deceptively simple: You must ensure that your Ideal Customers make an investment in their relationship with you, and you must make certain that walking away from the relationship also means walking away from the investment. Their investment can be financial, operational or even emotional. It can be visible or invisible. It can be tangible or intangible. But it must exist and it must be made known to your customer.

Customer retention is not driven by how much it cost your Ideal Customers to *use* you, customer retention is driven by how much it costs your Ideal Customers to *lose* you. Ask yourself what it would cost your best customers to walk away from you this very day. If the answer is either, "not much," or, "I don't know," then you are in a perilous relationship with your best customers and you must make some changes. (Thank goodness for Step 1!)

In business school, this important strategy of customer investment is referred to as establishing switching costs—costs that your customers would incur if they switched to one of your competitors. Large businesses take great pains to introduce switching costs into their key relationships. Dot-com companies give away access to their sites, hoping to establish customer retention. Airlines give away frequent flyer miles and first class upgrades so that there is a cost associated with defecting to their competitors. (A "cost" such as having to sit in coach instead of first class or of not accruing miles for that Hawaii vacation.) Car washes give the tenth wash free. Phone companies make their rates impossible to compare with others, which makes switching as complex as possible. Credit card companies rebate a percentage of expenditures in cash. Leasing companies impose financial penalties for early termination. Printers keep your original artwork. Suppliers give volume discounts. Physicians keep your medical records, and so on.

Small business owners, however, are so often so obsessed with their own expenditures, that they miss the true nature of switching costs. While they focus on the investment of time and money *they* have made in acquiring a new customer (sales and marketing, evaluations, presentations, prototypes, etc.), what really matters is the investment of time and money that *their customer* has made in them! While I'm sure that some of your customers are really nice people, the truth is, they don't care how much the relationship costs you, they care how much it costs them.

For example, if you sink $10,000 into a new machine in order to better serve a new customer, they could still walk away tomorrow and justify it as a "business decision." But if *they* sunk $10,000 into that new machine, walking away would be a much more difficult decision, wouldn't it?

Your customer's investment in the relationship with you should come early on (beginning in the pre-sales phase), and should continue throughout the lifecycle. The greater their investment, the less likely they are to leave you, and, as we will see in Step 5, the greater opportunity you will have for maximum profitability. Their investment can be in cash (large consulting firms often require payments in advance merely for the evaluation phase) or in time and materials. After all, both time and materials can ultimately be converted to a cash value.

If five of your prospective customer's employees sit through three of your pre-sales presentations (each being three hours in length), then they have just invested 45 man-hours—*before* making a decision to enter into a relationship. The cost per man-hour could vary widely, but even at a modest fully burdened rate of $35, merely attending your sales presentations effectively cost your prospective customer $1,575. And that figure does not include travel, or the time that these individuals may invest evaluating your information before and after that particular presentation. The only way for them to recoup their investment, is to do business with you. If they do not do business with you, they will have to incur additional costs to evaluate other prospective suppliers.

Estimating switching costs requires an understanding of the true costs associated with the use of the various products or services you offer, many of which are not obvious. Suppose I developed a new word processing software package that clearly surpasses Microsoft Word in ease of use and capability. And, hoping to establish market share, suppose I offer my product to major corporations free of charge. How many Microsoft Word users do you think will take advantage of this free offer?

Hopefully, you said few. Or, perhaps even none. And hopefully you gave this answer because it's intuitively obvious to you that the "true cost" of switching from Microsoft Word is not at all related to the price of the product. The true cost of switching is hidden in the thousands of hours already invested in its use. The true cost is in the retraining that would be required to adopt a new standard. The true cost is in the risk that thousands of archived files might no longer be compatible, and that myriad other programs might not interface seamlessly. The true cost is the risk of the long-term viability and support presented by the newcomer…the uncertainty.

Why should anyone accept this level of risk? Who would knowingly incur these actual and potential costs? Almost no one would, as Microsoft (and the Justice Department) so clearly knows. The costs of switching are just too high, and they get higher each time we sit down and create a new document using Microsoft Word.

A few years ago, several software companies ran national advertising campaigns offering their money management software free for the asking. More than a million people took them up on their offer. How did these companies expect to ultimately profit from this deal? Through switching costs. They hoped that once their software was received, potential customers would open it, load it onto their computers, learn how to use it, input some data and play around. In other words, they would invest their time. And time is money. Not everyone, of course, would decide to use the software on a long-term basis. But some would, and those new customers would begin to pay for upgrades, supplies, add-ons, etc. Once roots are established in this way, it is far easier to grow your columns of revenue up and to introduce new products and services for existing customers.

Keep in mind that the Lifetime Value of a Customer (LV/C) mentioned in Step 3 continues to play a vital role in determining the degree of switching costs necessary. In this case, being able to estimate how many years a customer would continue to use this money management software (assuming an upgrade every year) was crucial to knowing how much to invest in the pre-sales campaign.

Typically, it is helpful to think of switching costs as coming in three broad categories:

1) Pre-sale and acquisition
2) Start-up and learning curve
3) Takedown and replacement.

Taking The Other Side

You might want to read the following descriptions twice. The first time, try to put yourself in the mind of your Ideal Customer, and ask whether these costs presently exist for them. If so, try to estimate a dollar value. Remember, time is money, so this may require multiplying man-hours times an estimated wage rate, as in the example above. The second time through, brainstorm (perhaps with others in your organization) whether any of these costs can be *increased*. For example, once you recognize that time spent training your customers is an investment by *both* of you, and you have quantified that investment, you might want to consider significantly *increasing* the training you require. Doubling the training time required, for example, would double your customer's early stage investment. While your investment would also increase, this should be easily recovered over time through the extended protection against competition, and the greater LV/C that the additional investment on their part induces.

Now, let's look at the three types of switching costs, beginning with pre-sale and acquisition costs. Even in point-of-sale environments such as retail and restaurants, the sale ordinarily begins long before the customer walks through the door and places the credit card on the counter. This is even truer of professional service and manufacturing concerns. For every sale you make, there was an antecedent in the form of an advertisement, phone call, referral, sales presentation, proposal, feasibility study, etc. Depending on your business, there may even have been prototypes or limited production runs. Most entrepreneurs tend to focus on the out-of-pocket costs to their firm during these stages. But, keep in mind that there is someone on the other end receiving, analyzing, discussing, evaluating and comparing that same information. Even in the earliest phases of the customer/supplier acquisition process, a *mutual* investment has begun, and the smart entrepreneur will consciously control the size and scope of the prospective customer's investment.

Philosophically, this implies that the greater the investment your customers make in the pre-sale and start-up phase, the greater their loyalty will be in latter phases. However, there is obviously a point beyond which they will not invest, so demanding too much of them could cast your competitors in a positive light. Discovering how far to push them at this early stage is as much art as science. And, while no formula exists for determining the ideal level of investment, it can be safely stated that, fearing rejection and craving revenue, most small business owners do not demand enough investment on the part of their Ideal Customers in the early phases.

The following is an example of the timid and short-term mindset:

"We can't invest much on pre-sale activities because we're tight on cash and might not get the job, and then we will have wasted all of that time and money, not to mention the opportunity costs of calling on other prospects. So, we'll quickly crank out a proposal...perhaps one that's mostly boilerplate from previous jobs. Then, we'll give them a price they can't refuse!"

This regrettably common mindset seeks to minimize out-of-pocket costs, including those masked as time. Yet in minimizing their own pre-sale investment, they have also minimized that of the prospective customer. Combined with the low price the customer is going to be offered, a worst-case scenario is born—a time-consuming, low-margin customer who has nothing invested and can change suppliers on a whim.

Now, consider the long-term mindset—the mindset of the entrepreneur who expects to convert each prospect into an Ideal Customer, and to keep them for an extended and profitable period of time:

"Since this prospect fits the profile of our Ideal Customer, we want to increase this prospect's investment during the pre-sale and start-up phases. In order to establish mutual commitment to the relationship, we will require extended participation by their top people. We may even ask for a retainer, or other form of advance, which could be applied to the job should they decide to go forward."

Loving The Difficult Sale

There is no question that the long-term mindset creates the more difficult sale. But difficulty of the sale often equates to the long-term retention and profitability of the customer. The fear of investing heavily to earn a sale (financially and emotionally) and then failing to do so, is what forces many entrepreneurs to repeatedly accept customers that have little or no long-term profit potential. An entrepreneur who demands no mutual investment by his customer, might acquire ten for every one that was required to invest. And that's the bad news! If these ten customers are accepted, your employees will spend all of their time and resources trying to satisfy (and retain) customers who have no commitment, no investment and no loyalty whatsoever to you. And, since your proposals were generic, you will no doubt discover that you have actually landed ten very different customers, who together will stretch and strain the resources of your small firm to the breaking point. Some years from now, if you survive, you will be trying to undo what was done in haste. (Think Diamond Courier and CRI from earlier steps.)

If, however, you have the courage to insist on mutual investment during the earliest phases, you will ensure yourself a period of strong profitability down the line. The Ideal Customer comes into the fold already committed and already invested. They have reasons *not* to walk away the first time a bump in the road is encountered. They have incentives to try and make the relationship work. If your prospects are not willing to mutually invest up front, it foreshadows how loyal they are likely to be over the long run. My advice is that you do not invest in them, either.

To increase the chances of a new customer eventually becoming a cash cow, their investment in you must continue during the start-up and learning curve phases. This investment can occur even if the customer is much larger than you are and has many alternative suppliers. Suppose, for example, that servicing a new customer requires the installation of specialized hardware and software in order to transact business in their preferred manner. On the surface, this might seem to be an investment on your part—the hardware, software and training. But the time your customer spent negotiating that agreement, training your people and helping with the installation, are all investments on their part. They might even pay for the hardware and software required if you ask them to. They now have a vested interest and want to see the relationship succeed. They do not want to have to go trough this exercise again and incur additional costs with a new vendor.

I've seen many small business owners decide that it was not worth all the effort that would be required to do business a certain way for a large customer. In fact, it may have been well worth it, since the odds of keeping that customer go up in proportion to the difficulty of making that transition. Bear in mind, that for switching costs to have impact, they must be known to the customer. And, while the customer may know the obvious ones (such as direct cash expenditures), there are many less obvious ones that you must make known to them. You must learn to brag on yourself in direct and indirect ways. For instance, if you have absorbed some costs, you should find a way to announce that fact to your customer. If you over-deliver by performing extra work but did not charge for it, at least send them an invoice stating the amount and mark it, "No Charge!" If these invoices are going to anonymous clerical people, then send a copy, FYI, to the decision makers. If you have added staff, purchased equipment or implemented training in order to serve them better, hold quarterly meetings to update them on your commitment. Wear T-shirts with their logos on them. Introduce them to your new, dedicated people. These meetings not only require the additional investment of time by your customer, but they make invisible costs visible. And only visible costs lead to customer retention.

As you and your Ideal Customer become more and more proficient at doing business together, their switching costs, or roots, will grow. And, as you become more and more efficient at doing business together, your profitability will grow.

Green Handcuffs

The ultimate motivation for your Ideal Customers to stay with you is that a "takedown," that is, the cost of replacing you, would be too great. As an example, suppose you have provided them with the equipment necessary to interact with you. This could include computers for order entry, machines for production, or simply reliance on some of your key employees for advice and support. Before switching suppliers they must consider the very real costs of replacing *all* that you have provided, which goes far beyond just the products and services they are billed for. They must accept that the cost of acquiring a new supplier will be at least what they have thus far invested in you. And they will know how much that is, because you will have repeatedly let them know!

Takedown costs, like all switching costs, can be strong or weak, but it is the cumulative total that matters. An example of a strong takedown cost would be a contractual penalty for terminating the relationship. A weak takedown cost might be the cookies that you send them each December. The objective is to identify and impose as many different switching costs as possible, so that the cumulative effect is strong. Why don't you take a moment right now to go back through the three categories above, and make a preliminary list of what costs your Ideal Customers incur by doing business with you. Then, consider how you might increase those costs. Remember, it is preferable to acquire *fewer* customers overall, so long as the ones you acquire become Ideal Customers.

Can you think of additional switching costs? This would be another great brainstorming session to hold with your people. Be creative. Don't just include marketing issues, as the fact that your customers spend time with someone in accounting may be a switching cost that you are not even aware of. Remember, you're searching for aspects of doing business with you that create investment on the part of your customer. Here are some ideas to get you started:

- Factory tours
- Tools or dies
- Travel
- Processes
- Entertainment
- Public Relations
- Gifts
- Awards
- Demonstrations
- Special terms
- Special reports or forms
- Rebates or volume discounts
- Quarterly update meetings
- Great service
- Events (golf tournaments, retreats, etc.)

It's Hot In Texas

Many entrepreneurs claim that a personal relationship with their customers is their greatest competitive advantage. And, while I have tried to point out that hard costs will ultimately retain more customers than warm and fuzzy costs, I do not want to discount the importance of the warm and fuzzies. During the time I was writing this chapter, the official temperature in Austin hit 110° and 112° on successive days. In other words, it's hot in the summer in Texas.

Yet dedicated runners, myself included, cannot be discouraged. And those of us who insist on running at five o'clock in the afternoon, invariably finish our runs dripping with sweat and well on the way to dehydration. Can you imagine how appreciative we are that someone has taken the time and trouble to place coolers full of sports drinks at the end of the running trail?

They're placed there courtesy of Paul Caroza, owner of Run-Tex, a local retail running store that sells mostly shoes and clothing. A former four-minute miler, Paul understands how to build customer loyalty. He doesn't consider it an imposition to make sure that coolers of water and sports drinks are made available every warm day of the year. There are no banners or brochures or advertisements. None are necessary. Believe me, the thirsty runners know who is refreshing them. And they know where they are going to buy their next pair of shoes, shorts, socks....

It's little things like this that have enabled Paul to overcome the intense competition in the athletic shoe market, and that have enabled him to open his fourth store in Austin. How can this entrepreneur dominate the market for running shoes in a large city—a city filled with huge discount shoe stores and specialty stores in malls? He can dominate because he understands focus (Step 8) and he has established benevolent switching costs. He has grown roots into his customer's psyche.

Think of the implications of that kind of loyalty. I estimate that I spend $1,000 per year at Run-Tex. If I continue to be blessed with good health, I would expect to continue that rate of spending (not adjusted for inflation) for the next 20 years. Thus, I'm worth at least $20,000 to Run-Tex over my lifetime—and this doesn't even include the many people each year whom I refer to Run-Tex. I suspect I am a fairly typical Run-Tex customer: I would not only drive farther to get to Paul's store, if necessary, but I would also pay more once I got there. I'm not saying that Paul's prices are high, I'm saying that because of the loyalty he has earned, I don't even bother to compare. I wouldn't care if I did have to pay more than I would pay at the big shoe store at the mall. Where were the Foot Locker folks when I was in need of a refreshing drink?

The Pig Was Committed

I'm going to buy from Paul Caroza. Period. End of discussion. That's the kind of retention you want to build within your customer base. So ask yourself, which of your customers feels that way about doing business with you and why? Can you instill that degree of loyalty within all of your Ideal Customers?

It is important to get creative about the concept of installing switching costs. I strongly suggest that a brainstorming exercise be undertaken including employees at all levels and I further suggest that you do this at a retreat. Get out of your office. Get into casual clothes. Go out to a lake, or a mountain, or a hill, or a beach, or whatever removes you from the constriction of the office environment. Take a look at the multiple points of contact between you and your customer. You may be surprised at the level of crucial contacts, such as how your customers enjoy speaking to your receptionist. If you were to replace that friendly receptionist with a cold and unfriendly voice-mail system, you might, in fact, be reducing the switching costs for your customers, thereby making it just a bit easier for them to leave you. Put a value on that. Find a way to make that value visible to your customers. (And don't forget to let your receptionist know that he or she is playing an important role on your team.)

In conclusion, growing roots is all about changing your viewpoint from how much you are investing in a customer relationship, to how much the customer is investing in you. It's about realizing that customer satisfaction does not equate to customer retention, and that customer retention is the key strategy of the profitable firm.

I am reminded of the old story of a ham and egg breakfast, used to depict the difference between involvement and commitment. They hen, as they say, was involved in the breakfast, while the pig was committed. Satisfied customers may be *involved*, but customers who are retained through switching costs are *committed*, and your profits will come from their commitment.

Photo Map Update

The fourth area of development for your photo map is that of health and fitness. I use the two terms because to me, fitness results primarily from exercise and largely has to do with how we look. Health results mostly from practices related to diet and lifestyle and contributes to how we feel. Both are important, even those elements that others would consider vain. Many 8-steps graduates select images of people they consider fit and attractive.

And how can your business contribute to these goals? First, follow the rule of "do no harm." Less is more. As Thoreau said, "Simplify, simplify." In other words, don't let unnecessary complexity and the drive for survival, create stress in your life. Working only with Ideal Customers is a way to create a business model that provides the time and the emotional rewards that contribute to your health. Nothing else in your future will be as enjoyable as you deserve if your health is suffering. Really, this area should be first in everyone's mind.

Pricing For Profit

Step 5

Wavering between the profit and the loss
In this brief transit where the dreams cross

—T.S. Eliot

Sales and marketing often dominate the thoughts and actions of entrepreneurs. To prove my point, just look at the onslaught of books, seminars and consultants that proliferate in that field. Perhaps this is because most entrepreneurs, no matter how great their idea, learn early on that they must have the fortitude to sell before their fledgling business has a chance of getting off the ground.

But at some point during a company's growth, often sooner than one would expect, continuing to focusing on sales and marketing activities becomes a detriment if the entire business model is not working efficiently. At some point, the same entrepreneur who survived by making sales will actually begin to damage his or her company by making *more* sales. These same entrepreneurs, however, often spend a great deal of time and money trying to get themselves and their sales representatives, motivated to sell *more*. Then, when they're successful in selling more, they bemoan the lack of cash in their business.

To grow requires cash. If you don't have a cash-efficient business model, generating more sales is certain to threaten your business. And, don't think you're going to stroll into the bank and obtain a working capital line of credit just because your sales are growing. That's not the type of working capital that banks like to finance. In fact, they will probably tell you that you are growing *too fast*. (I know, just last week they told you that you were not growing fast enough.)

When I'm conducting an 8-steps workshop, I frequently compare an entrepreneur who thinks more sales will solve all problems to a person digging his own grave. If your business model is not cash-efficient, then firing up your troops to sell more is tantamount to asking them to dig the grave *faster*. While I'm in favor of training, and a fan of many motivational materials, I fear that too often so-called marketing experts know little or nothing about what constitutes a cash-efficient business model.

Call me old-fashioned, but if I see someone digging their own grave, I normally suggest that they do two things as quickly as possible. First, I suggest they *stop digging*. Secondly, I suggest they climb out of the hole so that by intelligently examining their business model, they can determine where to better spend the energy that was being spent digging the grave.

If you'd like to stop digging and radically increase your revenues, profits and cash flow (with virtually no additional effort), I have a quick and easy solution for you: Raise your prices.

Can you do that? Is it that easy? Don't your competitors and your desired market share dictate prices? Won't all of your customers leave if you raise your prices?

To a degree, of course, prices are influenced by outside forces. But I think it is philosophically more important for the business owner to view prices as the result of controllable, *internal* factors, rather than to throw up his hands to the whims of the so-called market. In my experience with thousands of small business owners, almost all of them underprice their offerings and few would lose customers by pricing higher. Since the increase in prices goes straight to the bottom line, the results of even small changes in pricing strategy can be astounding.

Price vs. Cost

To consistently price low, it would be necessary for a small business to be the low-cost leader, and few small businesses can or should strive to be low-cost leaders in their fields. Among the many small business men and women who think of themselves as low-cost leaders, most are confusing cost with price. Just because a mom-and-pop operation has low overhead (the proverbial kitchen table) they may *think* that offering a lower price than a big company means that they are the low-cost provider. They are wrong. It only means that, probably out of some form of fear or desperation, they are willing to give up profits on a particular job in order to get a sale. This is a short-term strategy certain to keep one's head bobbing just above and below the surface of success. True low-cost positions are required to pursue low-price strategies and low-cost positions usually demand access to large amounts of capital and large economies of scale. In other words, low-cost strategies are seldom available to small firms.

Let's take Southwest Airlines, for example. Southwest Airlines typically offers the lowest fares on most of its routes. They have a reputation as a low-*price* leader—a true value as represented by their famous commercial in which their fares and their meals are both represented by a bag of peanuts. (I can't resist mentioning another great Southwest ad in which they say that they would like to match American Airlines' new low fares…except that they would have to *raise* theirs!)

I'm pleased when someone in a workshop points out that Southwest does not *always* offer the lowest fares on all routes. This gives me the opportunity to explain that a low-cost position does not mean that the company must pass on those savings to their customers. Just because they are the low-cost leader, Southwest does not also have to be the low-price leader. Rather, they have *chosen* to be the low-price leader, a strategy that is sustainable only if they remain the low-*cost* provider. Please keep these distinctions clear in your mind. In fact, it's best to make the philosophical stretch that cost and price have no relationship to each other, except as they independently affect the bottom line.

Also recognize that becoming the low-cost provider has nothing to do with marketing, though its advantages may be communicated through the marketing channel. For Southwest Airlines, becoming the low-cost provider has to do with a huge investment in infrastructure, operations, logistics and training, so that they can fly one seat, one mile, for less than their competitors. The ability to sustain a cost advantage in the market place is largely a result of controllable, internal strategies. The fact that Southwest then *chooses* to pass on those savings to its customers, that is, to be the low-*price* competitor, is a strictly arbitrary decision on the part of their CEO, and is merely communicated to the public through the marketing process.

In fact, while I am in no way trying to diminish the importance of marketing, I think an appropriate distinction is that it is the responsibility of marketing to communicate to customers the strategic advantages and value proposition of a firm. But those advantages, and that value proposition, cannot just be pulled out of thin air. They are the basis for sustained profitability and are created by the *entirety* of serious solutions that create a working business model throughout every functional area of a company—large or small.

Southwest Airlines is able to offer low fares because of its brutally efficient operations, as evidenced by the rapid turnaround of its planes. Wal-Mart is able to offer low prices because of its enormous procurement advantages and powerful information systems. Dell Computer is the master at wrenching profits from custom orders with its direct-to-customer model. Any of the CEOs of these firms (whose primary job is the development of strategy) would find it horrifying if their marketing departments were off developing new pricing strategies independent of the very nature of the company's assets and investments.

Yet that is exactly what many small business owners unintentionally do: They look for a new marketing strategy, value proposition or sales campaign without the proper consideration of their own assets and investments. They spend too much time conveying the "benefits" of their business model without having created a model to actually *deliver* those benefits. They speak of "perceived" value without the awareness that perceived value is sustainable only if it is also true value. This often results in digging the grave faster. They are in a mad dash to fulfill promises they made but which their business model is not prepared to keep.

The Magic Of Pricing

Which brings us back to pricing. Pricing is a powerful and highly leveraged tool—a tool that all business owners have within their reach. Properly understood and applied, pricing can have an almost magical effect on the bottom line—and those effects can occur almost instantly. Let's do some goal setting for a moment by looking at a very simplified income statement and business model:

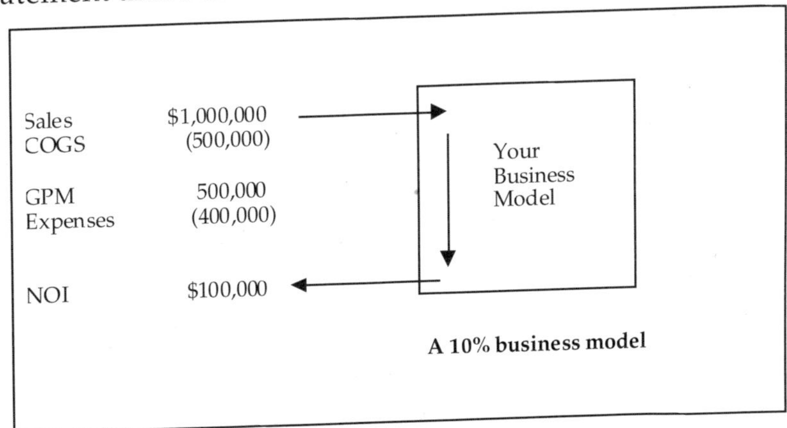

A 10% business model

Please put your consultant's hat back on and think of how you could double the net operating income (NOI) of this business. I have asked over a thousand business students and business owners that question and over 80% of the responses begin with the knee-jerk reaction to double sales. The assumption is that this is a 10% business model (10% of gross sales work their way down to the pre-tax income line, or NOI) and that the rules of this 10% model must be followed.

I then ask my students and entrepreneurs what changes will have to be made in order for this small company to generate and support a doubling of sales. They acknowledge it will likely be necessary to double the sales force, double the amount of inventory (adding space to hold it), adding customer support and order entry personnel, increasing utility, insurance and other overhead expenses. In other words, not only must sales double, but so must the overall complexity of the business. And, it may take a year or more for the bottom line changes to completely ripple through.

When I ask these same entrepreneurs if they would like to double net operating income, almost all say that they would. However, when I ask them if they are excited about taking on the added complexity and management headaches just described, most say that they are not. Most express some concern about whether it is worth the added complexity and risk to gain the added profits. And, while this debate can elicit a wide variety of responses, I normally preempt it with another question, far easier to answer.

How, I ask, would they like to double NOI without adding *any* additional complexity, or expense? How would they like to double NOI with no additional effort?

Hands fly into the air.

It couldn't be simpler, I tell them—change your pricing strategy. And no, you don't have to raise prices 100% like you would an increase in sales *volume*. In fact, based on the model above, you would only have to raise your prices 10% in order to double NOI. That's the leverage of pricing. Every penny of increase goes straight into your pocket.

When you merely raise your prices, nothing else changes. The only added expense you incur is changing your catalog or price list. You don't have to handle more inventory since unit sales remain the same. You have no additional customers. You need no additional space or personnel. Your business is no more complex than it was the day before—just more profitable. And you don't have to wait a year for the results to trickle in. They will start to be felt after the very next sale. Incredibly, a 10% price increase in the model shown earlier in this chapter would look like this:

	Before	**After**	**Effect**
Sales	$1,000,000	$1,100,000	Up 10%
COGS	-$500,000	-$500,000	No change
GPM	$500,000	$600,000	Up 20%
Expenses	-$400,000	-$400,000	No change
NOI	$100,000	$200,000	Up 100%

Doubling NOI With a 10% Price Increase

Changes in prices are best introduced by small businesses through simple tests. But for those who are interested, the leverage indicated in the example above is mathematically predictable. Here, we had a 10% net profit margin. (Profit divided by total sales.) If we divide the number 1 by our net profit margin (1/10) we will have calculated the impact of a 1% increase in prices. In this case, a 1% increase in prices resulted in a 10% increase to the bottom line. Since we raised prices 10% for this example, our NOI increased 100%.

If your net profit margin is 6%, a 1% increase in prices will yield an additional 17% increase in profits. (One divided by six.) If your net profit margin is 13%, a 5% increase in prices will yield a 38% increase in profits. (One divided by 13 times 5.) And so on. If your net profit margin is negative, the steps in this book should take care of that in short order. For now, you can use a *projected* net profit margin to evaluate the impact of future changes in pricing.

Just remember: Pricing Impact = 1/npm

Dear Mr. Greenspan

Before I get e-mails from the economists among my readers, let me say that, yes, I studied micro- and macroeconomics in college. I'm well aware of the concept of the price elasticity of demand. I'm sure that Alan Greenspan could point to some flaws in my assumption that an increase in prices, however small, will not result in lost customers, thus negating the net effect of our price increase. And to Mr. Greenspan I would say: "Tell me again how many *small* businesses you've run?"

These economic principles, like the laws of physics, do establish *theoretical limits* as to what the market will bear. But to assume that a small business owner is already pricing to the optimum limits of economic theory, is, well...let's just say, not likely. There are limits to how fast objects on earth can move without burning up due to friction, but even gold medal sprinters don't spend a lot of time worrying about this fact.

The concept of price elasticity of demand means that, in theory, if you raise prices, demand for your products and services will go down. The economists seek to mathematically predict the precise impact by employing the formula:

$PE = \%\Delta q / \%\Delta p$

Or, % change in quantity demanded divided by % change in price.

What does this mean? It means that if a 2% increase in price results in a 10% fall in demand, the price elasticity of demand would be -10/2 = -5. If demand falls 2% with a 2% increase in price, the elasticity is said to be -1.

This is important, not because you will ever have to calculate this number, but because you do need to understand that the *less* elastic the demand for your products and services, the more it pays for you to attempt to raise your prices. Much of what I'm trying to accomplish through these 8 steps is to make the demand for your products and services less price elastic. Lower price elasticity will enable you to raise your prices without losing customers, which will have a profound impact on your bottom line profits.

You can put the factors that allow you to charge higher prices to work for you immediately, so let's consider them now:

1) Relatively few direct competitors or substitute goods;
2) Your customers don't notice price increases;
3) Your customers are reluctant to change their habits or search for new suppliers;
4) Your customers see additional benefits associated with the price increases—your value proposition remains intact.

This is why price increases are more art than science and why they so clearly demonstrate whether other aspects of your competitive strategy are working. Obviously, if you have carefully recruited your Ideal Customers and built in switching costs, your ability to increase prices will be enhanced. Let's consider these four pricing factors one-by-one and see how you can put them to work for you.

1) Relatively few direct competitors or substitute goods. We will look at this much more closely in Step 8, but I will tell you in advance that it is crucial for the small business owner to differentiate their products and services from competitors in the minds of their Ideal Customers. The most important question you can ask about your business is what makes it unique. In other words, you must do whatever is necessary to avoid *direct* comparison with competitors. Whether through branding, niche marketing or stellar service, it is vital that you prevent your Ideal Customers from making a one-on-one comparison of you versus a potential competitor.

Some business owners tell me that they find this difficult, that there are hundreds of businesses listed in the yellow pages "just like" theirs. I tell them that there are also dozens of brands of toothpaste, toilet paper, detergent and even water at my supermarket, and if water can be differentiated, so can their products and services. Your goal should be to establish such a high degree of uniqueness that there are no *direct* competitors and no substitute goods. This would also mean that your prices are less elastic and can be increased with a high level of confidence that your customers will not abandon you.

2) Your buyers don't notice the price increases.

There are many ways, subtle and direct, to increase prices without notice by your Ideal Customers. I once consulted with a manufacturer of board games. They shipped about 80,000 games a year at $39.95 each. To increase their profits (which were only about $100,000 a year) I strongly advocated a price increase. But the owner felt that exceeding the "$40 barrier" would reduce sales (price elasticity) and insisted on keeping his prices where they had been for seven years. He had no evidence to support this "gut feel."

As a compromise, I suggested he add $1 to shipping and handling. He had no problem with that (he didn't know what the actual cost was anyway), did not lose a single customer that I am aware of, and increased his net profit by a whopping $80,000 a year, or 80%! This was a completely invisible net price increase to the customer

U-Haul offers its trucks at near break-even prices. In fact, when competitors compete fiercely on price, U-Haul will even provide trucks at a loss. Why? Because they don't make money on trucks—they make money on supplies. And when they lose a little bit on the trucks, they just mark up the price of blankets, dollies, boxes and tape. The customer, focused on the easily comparable truck rental rates, scarcely notices the total bill. And U-Haul has designed its entire business model to make sure that not only the prices, but also the gross profit margins of its supplies are spectacular.

I had Stanley Steemer clean my carpets not long ago. They did a super job for about $100. Being insatiably curious about business models, I tried to mentally calculate the cost of their truck and their two-man team for two hours. I determined, at best, they had a gross profit margin on that job of about $20. As they were leaving, they talked to me about a pet stain on my carpet. They convinced me that I should let them put a chemical on the stain that would kill the lurking bacteria and, hopefully, discourage repeat visits by my dog. Though I had managed to stave off their offers of Scotch Guard and furniture cleaning, I gave in to the stain treatment. That cost was $50 and the process took about 3 minutes. Gross profit? I would estimate about $49.50—more than tripling the total gross profit for the original job. The consumer in me cringed. The business professor in me quietly applauded.

Have you ever been offered a warranty agreement at the counter where you purchased an electronic device? Consider that a net price increase. There is no end to the creative ways you can effectively increase your prices. A good first step is to deconstruct your current offerings—that is, break everything that you provide your customer down into the smallest possible increments. (Products, service, installation, training, delivery, etc.) Then, try and assign the fair portion of the total price to each and see if unbundling, or bundling differently, would allow you to price differently, including some invisible increases.

While teaching you about electronic spreadsheets is beyond the scope of this book, I would be remiss if I didn't mention how powerful it is to have your business model—complete with deconstructed pricing—set up as a spreadsheet model. Not until you are able to quickly run through a wide variety of "What if?" scenarios will you be able to experience the full jaw drop that price sensitivity analysis often creates.

By the way, this concept of knowing which of the various columns of revenue (trucks or supplies in the case of U-Haul) produce the lion's share of profits is sometimes referred to as "profit pools." Ford Motor Company receives only about 10% of its total revenues (sales) from leasing, yet that "pool" of revenue has produced almost half of the company's profits in certain years. Can you see how this information could, and almost certainly has, changed the entire strategy of that firm? If the profits are in leasing, then it would make sense to sell the maximum number of cars possible, even at prices near (or theoretically below) the break-even point.

Jewell Parker, an 8-steps workshop graduate, owns a meeting facility business. Where do you think she makes the majority of her profit—in renting space, renting equipment or catering? Well, I'm not going to tell you the answer, but what do you think her strategy should be if her profit pool is in equipment rental, for example? I hope you said that she should price the meeting space well below market (or give it away) and offer free cookies to those who rent lots of equipment.

Some people don't like the term "loss leader" because it sounds manipulative, but it's really not if you think about it. What's wrong with a grocery store offering a modern-day staple like Coca-Cola for a ridiculously low price, knowing that you'll probably buy other things while you're there? Turning the light on my own industry for a moment, what's wrong with offering to speak for below market rates, or to conduct workshops for free, if the speaker knows from experience that a certain number of attendees will buy his books, tapes and other products at the back of the room?

How does Peter Lowe, the motivational impresario, pay $50,000 apiece to bring the top speakers in the country to your city (Colin Powell, George Bush, etc.) and yet charge you only $35? How do cellular phone dealers manage to give away the phones? Why are so many companies trying to give away PCs if you agree to two years of Internet access through their network?

One 8-steps workshop graduate installs computer networks. His company used to bundle hardware, software and training into one price. But, with the price of comparable hardware so easily accessible, he found that their customers were price shopping. While we've established that direct comparison is not desirable, it is sometimes unavoidable and his customers thought he was charging too much for the hardware. So, my client unbundled his offering and *lowered* the price of his hardware to below market, thereby gaining more sales. At the same time he *increased* the price of training, which he also made sure to present to his customers as the absolute best in the industry. The total price of an average installation was actually *increased*, as was the overall profitability, yet the customer had the perception of a greater value than before.

Deconstruct your product and service offerings. Break them down into as many discrete components as possible and then brainstorm various pricing strategies. How can you maximize *profits*? Do you have one revenue column that is unusually profitable? (Like Ford's leasing?) Is there a way that you can lure customers into that column, perhaps by discounting items and services contained in nearby columns? Be creative. Think strategically. Think cumulative profits not total sales.

Another example of an invisible price increase is holding a price constant, while reducing that which is being delivered. (The cost to serve.) Do you really notice whether the net weight of your favorite cereal has gone down by an ounce even as the price remains the same? Or, whether your brand of toilet paper now has 30 fewer sheets? I recently noticed that my favorite brand of frozen waffles proclaimed on the box that they had "increased" each package from eight waffles to ten—more than enough to justify a small price increase. It was only when I got home that I noticed the net weight had not changed. I was paying more for ten small waffles, instead of eight larger ones. Think back to Step 3 and, in particular, the Cash Cow quadrant. In that crucial phase, the prices you charge your Ideal Customers may remain the same (or continue to increase slightly), but your cost to serve declines. The net difference is all increased profitability for you, and it all goes straight to the bottom line with no additional effort on your part.

3) Buyers are reluctant to change their habits or search for new suppliers.

This is all about switching costs and customer retention and thus, I will refer you to Step 4 if you would like a review. Suffice it to say that if buyers are satisfied *and* fully invested (and you've done your job by making them aware of that investment), then price increases, even if direct and noticeable, are not likely to make them rush out and start incurring the costs of finding new suppliers. The deeper you have grown your roots into your customer's organization, the greater will be their reluctance to change their habits.

4) Buyers see benefits associated with the increases—the value proposition remains intact.

Why not make a price increase a welcome and exciting event to your Ideal Customer? First, you may have been doing many things for the customer in the past that they never noticed and you never made visible to them. So, consider making a presentation to them detailing all that you do for them, showing them the additional value they are getting in return for a modest increase in price. Your customers raise the prices they charge their customers and should have no objection to your doing likewise. Just make sure to point out all of the wonderful things you are doing for them in return.

With these four areas handled properly, you will be better off forgetting about the theoretical aspects of the price elasticity of demand. With a proper business model, there will be precious few, if any, customers lost as a result of consistent, strategic price increases. The fear that often causes us to leave our profits in the pockets of our customers is usually ego-driven, not business-driven. What causes most small business owners to underprice is not so much that they must match so-called "market prices," but rather the emotional fear of rejection. Your ability to increase prices is one of the most powerful mirrors you have in which to view the viability of your business model. If you truly can't raise prices without losing customers, you have a tenuous business model at best. When you can raise prices without customer defections, then the lifetime financial goals that you're going to set in Step 7 will be imminently achievable.

If you've identified and grown roots within your Ideal Customer, they'll give you plenty of notice when your price increases are pushing them closer to the point of considering alternatives. (Their indifference point.) However, since that point cannot be mathematically predicted, you *must* steadily push them toward that point, which can also be thought of as the point of optimal profitability—the point at which your Ideal Customers might consider replacing you but would not actually do so. Anything less means that you are foregoing profits that you have rightfully earned, which is tantamount to giving an unintended cash rebate to your customers.

A *Harvard Business Review* article points out that the big drug company, Glaxo, introduced its Zantac ulcer medication to the U.S. market in 1983. The leader in this category was the five-year-old Tagamet. Since Zantac offered several advantages, Glaxo had the courage not to play follow-the-leader pricing despite a low-cost position. Instead, they priced Zantac 50% *higher* than Tagamet, positioning it in the customers' minds as a superior product. Within four years, Zantac became the market leader despite its higher price. (Or was it *due to* its higher price?) The same article, however, points out that Northern Telecom developed a superior telephone system but that the advantages were not clear to customers. A premium price in this case, would have devastated sales. Instead, they decided to introduce the system at a highly competitive price, and then educate customers as to the superiority, develop switching costs, and, later, reclaim profits through add-ons and new system sales.

Get a Cow

There is no practical way for a small business to precisely determine price elasticity, other than to test. You can even test different approaches with different customers as the big companies do. One major credit card issuer tests over a thousand different permutations of their basic offer every year. One that was surprisingly successful was developed exclusively for the Nebraska marketplace. The offer? "Get a card, get a cow." That's right, they gave a cow to everyone who applied for and was issued one of their credit cards...and the results were bullish.

You can even "risk" certain customers by trying out a new pricing strategy on ones that you wouldn't mind losing. If you are pricing at less than what your customer is willing to pay, you are foregoing profits you have *earned*, probably because your ego fears being rejected. There is no other way than to test, test and test some more. Then, test some more. Play with pricing.

As incentive for you to brainstorm the many easy and powerful ways to raise *net* prices, why don't you have some fun right now. Using your own net profit margin (pre-tax) why don't you do some "what-if" analysis and see how much a 1%, 5% or even a whopping 15% price increase would affect your bottom line. I suspect that when you remember those dollars go directly into your pocket, without any additional business (or life) complexity, you'll be anxious to get to work.

Photo Map Update

As you know by now, I believe there is great power in simplicity. Simply elegant are two words that I like to apply to great business models. I also believe we add power to our life's goals and aspirations if we can simplify them.

One exercise that has proven valuable in 8-steps workshops involves the development of a brief statement describing what you hope will be your enduring legacy. The best way to do this is to write a simple epitaph or obituary headline. I know this sounds depressing, but it can actually be fun. All you're trying to do is answer—briefly—the question: How would you like people to remember you? What would you like for them to say about you after you're gone?

Think about it and then see if you can find an image to remind you of this core essence of your life.

Breaking Out!

First say to yourself what you would be;
And then do what you have to do.

—Epictetus

One of the greatest myths inadvertently perpetuated by bankers and small business advisers is that a business owner should strive to break even. I suppose the logic behind this is that breaking even is better than failing, but I'm not sure that's true.

Now *passing* the break-even point like a rocket ship breaking free of Earth's atmosphere, is clearly reason for celebration. But what I see all too often, are businesses lingering near the break-even point for month after month and year after year. That is a terrible life to lead as a break-even existence does not provide the excess cash necessary to enjoy life, yet may also not cause enough pain to force the necessary changes. By comparison, at least outright failure forces the necessary corrections and changes. Hanging around the break-even point can be like being on life support…for years.

The principles that drive break-even analysis, however, can be extremely useful to project not only what you must do to survive in business, but what you must do to thrive and pay for all of your lifetime goals.

The break-even point of any business is where revenue (sales) = total costs, or;

$$\text{Revenue} = \text{TC}$$

That's not exactly rocket science, is it?

But if we deconstruct this equation slightly, we will give ourselves more variables to work with and more levers to pull as we begin our "what if?" analysis. Revenue is the result of a certain quantity of items (q) being sold at a certain price (p). For those in service businesses, remember that hours can also be considered as items. I often advise professionals to imagine their hours as "units," sitting on shelves as if they were books or software packages.

For the purposes of break-even analysis, total costs (TC) are divided into two types—fixed and variable. Before your eyes glaze over thinking that I'm getting ready to discuss arcane accounting concepts, let me assure you that is not the case. The ability to determine whether a cost is fixed or variable reflects an understanding crucial to owners and managers who hope to devise profitable strategies. Different types of costs may be defined by accountants, but they are exploited by strategists.

Think of fixed costs as those that, in the near term, would remain in place even if you had no sales. (e.g., rent, utilities, wages, etc.) Variable costs are those you incur only if and when you actually sell goods and services. (Commissions, freight…the cost of materials or direct labor, etc.)

And, since revenue = quantity x price, and total costs = fixed costs + variable costs, then break even occurs where:

$$\text{qty x price} = \text{fixed costs} + \text{variable costs, or;}$$

$$q \times p = fc + vc$$

This equation assumes that "vc" represents *total* variable costs, so it could be further deconstructed to variable costs *per unit* x the number of units, or:

$$q \times p = fc + (vc \text{ per unit}) \times q$$

Very quickly, you can probably see a number of ways to valuably exploit this simple equation. Those who are familiar with spreadsheet programs are probably envisioning a sensitivity analysis—a matrix or grid of possible outcomes based on varying assumptions. Being able to quickly change price, quantity and the ratio of fixed to variable costs (as well as their nominal amounts) will generate an astonishing number of very different bottom line results. Whether an electronic spreadsheet is employed, or lots of pencils are used, once the most profitable combinations of variables are obtained, it then behooves management to convert these "what if?" calculations into a discussion about the strategies that would be necessary to obtain those particular results.

Not All Fixed Costs Are Bad

The reason I see so many business owners turned off to break-even analysis is that it is often misused. For example, many managers latch onto the fact that lowering fixed costs will lower their break-even point. If breaking even is good, the thinking goes, then lowering fixed costs must be good. But this line of thinking is dangerously short sighted. For example, payroll is often the largest fixed cost for many small firms, and, if you are determined to reduce the payroll in order to reduce fixed costs, guess whose paycheck usually gets cut first? *Yours!* Is there something wrong with that logic? When the net worth of the owner and the business are shared, what is there to gain by increasing the value of one while reducing the value of the other? Other reductions in fixed costs can also be crippling. In an effort to reach break even as quickly as possible you might eliminate or reduce insurance, utilities, sales and marketing investments, research and development, training, or other recurring expenditures that will reduce costs in the short-term, but only at the expense of long-term success.

Now, let's put the basics of break-even analysis to use in a powerful way, keeping in mind that a few simple accounting distinctions can take your decision-making skills to a new level. You can use this tool not merely to find the break-even point for your business, but to find the *break-out* point for letting your business fund your personal goals and ambitions. Don't define your break-even point as a textbook would (where total revenues equal total costs), but rather define it as the level of sales (calculated in either dollars or units) necessary to sustain the growth of your business and finance your lifetime dreams. After all, dreams cost money and why else would you be working so hard?

One of my undergraduate students was researching this topic and discovered a story about a consultant, John Souerbry, who employed this approach. His client owned a golf shop and was himself, a fine golfer. In fact, the business owner's lifetime goal was to qualify for the PGA Senior Tour at age 50—only five years away. Rather than determining how much merchandise he needed to sell to "break even," or even to generate a modest profit, Souerbry had him calculate the expenses (travel, hotels, entry fees, etc.) that would be necessary to sustain him on the tour, even if winnings did not materialize.

The result showed that the business was not currently generating enough excess cash to fund the desired goals. Reaching the break-out point would require strong actions and new management strategies. Sales (or prices!) had to be increased and expenses trimmed. But by getting his head out of the sand and determining precisely what must be accomplished, the goal *was* achieved. It's amazing how often you can find a way to achieve something if you are crystal clear about what it is that you want to achieve—if you have a photographic image of it in your mind.

But even those who don't have a specific material goal for the day when work is optional can probably estimate a dollar amount. Would you feel comfortable retiring with $1 million in savings, or would $10 million be more like it? I'm assuming that whatever that number is for you, it must be built from the accumulation of "excess cash" produced by your business, less some terminal value attributed to the sale or liquidation of your business at some point in the future.

Forget Selling Your Business (For Now)

While on that subject, however, let me offer you a bit of stern advice based on years of experience: You will be much better off if you assume that your business will be worth *nothing* at the time you walk away from it. That's right, I said nothing. Zero. Nada. The reason I recommend this philosophical approach is that it is very often true, yet it catches those who have counted on a big nest egg from the sale of their business by surprise. It can leave them bitterly disappointed and far from financing their dreams. Let me explain.

I used to think a book dealing with the acquisition of lifetime goals would be difficult to write because those goals would vary so greatly among readers. Some entrepreneurs I've known, for example, have grand visions of luxurious second homes, while others envision charitable foundations bearing their names, and still others yearn for world travel. Others desire no outward manifestations of wealth at all.

But as I have put more and more business owners through 8-steps workshops and interviewed them for this book, I have become convinced that we all want one thing out of our work—we want for that work to be *optional*. And we want that day to come as soon as possible. We want to work — nobody works harder—we just don't want to *have* to work. When work is optional, some will opt to keep working. Others will work part time and still others will never work another moment in their lives. But what they all share, is that they want the decision of how much to work, and for how long, to be *their* choice, not a choice imposed on them by circumstances out of their immediate control.

Yet there are few instances where there is *less* control by the small business owner than when it comes time to sell his or her business. I could write an entire book on this topic, but for now, let me just forewarn of the factors that could dramatically reduce the value of your business. These include the economy, interest rates, the industry you are in, competition, technology, the vital role you play in the business and the mere fact that you operate a privately held concern. All of these things, and more, work to lower the value of your business. Time after time I have seen business owners disappointed—devastated even—when they realize that their firms are worth only a fraction of what they had believed. For them, the hopes and dreams they had imagined suddenly seem out of reach.

Building A Safety Net

But it doesn't have to be that way. There is a guaranteed safety net you can construct—creating excess cash through your business model. The more cash you have, the more options in life you have. You can leave the cash in your business, or take it out. You can invest in the stock market or buy a luxury car. You can pay yourself a bonus, provide profit sharing for your employees or give the money to your favorite charity. You can pay for your dreams. Without excess cash, however, none of these options is available to you.

Bill Gates and Warren Buffett are both multibillionaires with excess cash, yet their individual lifestyles vary greatly. Gates lives in an extravagant, opulent mansion, while Buffet lives in a modest middle-class home. For both men, work is an option, and they could freely choose to live the other's lifestyle if they preferred. They have options because they not only have cash, they have *excess* cash. Gates and Buffett have two other important advantages over most small business owners—advantages that extend beyond the sheer magnitude of their wealth. First, they traded their time (the only resource we are born with) to create companies that are now public, and which others would willingly pay them for. The approximate value of these public firms is known. This is rarely true for the small business owner.

Secondly, Gates and Buffett receive a portion of their excess cash from sources *other than* their primary business. They have diversified their sources of income, no matter how strongly they believe in their core business. They follow the Prudent Man Rule, which implores us not to keep all of our eggs in one basket. Do you?

Most small business owners are not so prudent, relying on their business as their *sole* source of cash. They rely on the cash produced by their business not only to pay normal company expenses, but also to pay for *personal* expenditures. While company financial statements and personal bank accounts may be technically separate, such things as home mortgage payments and college tuition effectively become invisible line items on the company's income statement, just as "fixed" as rent, wages and utilities. The retained earnings of their business, theoretically retained to finance business growth, are just as likely to fund a swimming pool for the family as a new truck for the company.

The greatest advice that I can offer to a business owner, then, is to use the techniques in this book to increase your cash to a point where "excess cash" can be taken *out of* your business and invested in other income-producing assets, eventually giving you multiple sources of cash. You can use the tools in this book to help clarify exactly how much excess cash you will need to finance your personal goals. And, once you know that number, you can tailor your business to produce that cash, day-by-day, without having to depend on the uncertainty of selling your business. If you are able to sell your business at some point in the future, consider that icing on the cake.

Another powerful approach to "break-out" budgeting is the contribution margin concept. This approach acknowledges that you have fixed and variable costs. Algebraically, it puts your fixed costs in the numerator, and your variable costs in the denominator. More important, it recognizes that most products and services have direct (variable) costs associated with them and what's left—the contribution margin—is what's available to cover the fixed costs of the company. Let's look at the formula where "/" means divided by:

Fixed costs = fc
Selling price per unit = sp_u
Variable costs per unit = vc_u
Break even = $fc / (sp_u - vc_u)$

Here's How It Works

Let's say that ABC Company sells a software product for $89 and that the variable costs of producing and shipping one unit are $10. Variable costs in this case would largely be the cost of the disks or CD, the printing of the manual, the packaging, handling, and shipping. Assuming fixed costs each month (rent, salaries, utilities, insurance, etc.) of $20,000, how many units does ABC have to sell to break even? Here's the math:

Fixed costs = $20,000
Selling price = $89
Variable cost per unit = $10

= $20,000 / ($89-$10)
= $20,000 / $79
= 253 units

ABC would have to sell 253 units a month to break even. But we don't want to break even, we want to *break out!* Suppose that the owner of this business needs $2,500 "excess cash" a month to build an adequate safety net. There are many scenarios that could lead to this and we want to find the best. A few of the questions this owner might ask are:

- How many units would have to be sold to generate $2,500 a month in "excess cash?"
- How many units would have to be sold to achieve this level of excess cash if prices were raised 10%? (Remember Step 5?)
- How many units would have to be sold to achieve this level of excess cash if prices were *lowered* 5%, yet fixed costs were reduced by $1,500 a month?
- Which would contribute more to profitability—lowering fixed costs or variable costs by 10%?

I could go on, and I hope you will, because these are the type of vital "what if?" questions that managers should be asking all the time. They are not questions that we should expect our accountants to raise, yet they intimately involve a basic understanding of break-even analysis and the nature of costs. In many cases, the answers can result in increased profitability without any changes to your basic business model, that is, no added complexity. The profits are there for the taking if you know where to look.

And by the way, here are the answers to the above questions:

- You would only have to sell 284 units a month to generate $2,500 a month in excess cash—an increase of 31 units a month, or about one a day. That doesn't sound too imposing, does it?
- You would only have to sell 256 units a month to generate $2,500 a month excess cash with a 10% price increase. That's little changed from the original volume of sales (253), once again showing the powerful impact of even a small price increase.
- You'd have to sell 281 units to generate $2,500 a month in excess cash if prices declined 5%, but fixed costs were cut by $1,500 per month;

• Cutting variable costs per unit by 10% would result in a break-even point of 250 units per month, while cutting fixed costs 10% would lower the break-even point to 228 units per month.

Give Me A Lever

When a manager realizes that the distribution of fixed and variable costs can impact not only the bottom line, but that it is also a strategic *choice*, the concept of operating leverage has been introduced. Many small business owners I meet use the term "leverage" but they often use it in relation to partnerships, strategic relationships or marketing—perhaps referring to word-of-mouth or networking. But in business school, leverage is a financial term—a quantifiable element of your business model that enables you to reap greater profits from each increased dollar of sales. If your sales go up 10%, and your profits also go up 10%, you are said to have no leverage—you're having to work just as hard for the last dollar of profit as you did for the first. If most of your costs are variable (the so-called "virtual" company) then you will have little or no leverage. This may be a safe place in bad times, but it can be a bad place in good times.

If, on the other hand, you properly construct a leveraged business model, it is entirely possible that, after a certain point, a 10% increase in sales will increase profits by 20%, 50%, or even more! Leverage is worth understanding and will drive home the importance of break-even (and break-out) analysis.

For this example, let's loosely define variable costs as those that you incur from third parties who are performing business operations on your behalf. In this case, you're importing clay pots from Mexico to resell. The cost of the pots is variable. Other variable costs include the commissions you pay your sales reps, the expense of your third-party packing and shipping, and the amounts paid to third-party bookkeeper and billing clerks.

While this approach can reduce risks (you incur no costs in the event of no sales), the problem is that everything you buy from others is priced to include their overhead—*and their required profit*. You are, in essence, paying full markup for every element of your product offering, and then marking it up again so that you may make a profit. The price of every product or service that you deliver to your customers, while perhaps containing only one overhead factor (your supplier's), has two profit markups. If you find yourself forced to compete on price, lowering your price will only wipe out *your* profit margin, not that of your suppliers.

But what if you were to convert some of your variable costs to fixed costs? What if, for example, you decided to make your own pots? Or, to hire a salary-based sales rep? Or, to hire and train your own shipping or billing clerk? How would that change your business model, and how would that affect your leverage and your bottom line? Let's find out through a simple example.

Suppose this clay pot company has sales of $100,000 and, operating as a "virtual company," has managed to keep all costs variable. Variable costs are 70% of sales, or $70,000. Since variable costs are also total costs in this case, the resulting net operating income (NOI) is $30,000, or 30% of sales. In the absence of any fixed costs, your break-even point is zero.

In Year Two, sales increase an impressive 20%, to $120,000. The more important question is how much did net operating income increase? One way to answer this is to multiply $120,000 times 70% and derive $84,000 (total costs) which when subtracted from $120,000 leaves $36,000. So, NOI increased by $6,000 which is also a 20% increase from the $30,000 of the previous year. Both sales and NOI increase 20%, indicating there is no operating leverage.

Another way to this answer this question is to know that operating leverage equals the change in NOI divided by the change in sales, or:

Δ NOI / Δ Sales

Obviously in this case, 20% (change in NOI) divided by 20% (change in sales) equals one, and, by definition, operating leverage of one means that this company has *no* operating leverage.

Now, let's look at this same company, assuming that you made a strategic decision (not an accounting decision!) to convert one half of all variable costs to fixed costs. Perhaps you hired a full-time pot maker and rented a small warehouse where the pots are made. Since it would be absurd to rent a facility that provided no room for growth, we can assume there is some excess capacity. And, given the pot maker's fixed salary, we can also assume that sales volume could increase substantially before having to hire a second pot maker.

In Year One, based on $100,000 in sales, you would have the same NOI as before—$30,000. But by understanding the *nature* of your costs, this time your variable costs were only 35% of total costs ($35,000) and your fixed costs were also 35%. Total costs were again $70,000 and NOI was again $30,000. On the surface, it looks the same.

But what do you think happens when you move to Year Two, and sales have again increased 20% to $120,000?

Variable costs remain at 35% of sales, or $42,000. But fixed costs did not go up at all! Since you have excess capacity, your fixed costs remained $35,000, resulting in total costs of $77,000 and NOI of $43,000! Sales went up 20%, but NOI went up 43%! (Operating leverage of 40/23 = 2.15.)

That's the power of operating leverage. Yet many business owners have been taught to think of leverage more as it relates to debt. That type of leverage—financial leverage—can have a similar positive impact on profitability, but it also has a major flaw in its application to small businesses. The flaw relates to the fact that few small business owners can arbitrarily create an optimal level of debt. With limited access to capital markets, they cannot always restructure existing debt on a whim, nor can they be sure of taking on more debt through bank loans.

The only point I want to make about financial leverage, therefore, is to say that debt is not necessarily bad, and that a carefully planned and optimal level of debt can have the same type of leveraged impact on your bottom line as an optimal level of fixed costs. I would encourage you to visit with your banker, or, if you don't have a banker, to find one and discuss your situation. The use of debt requires careful planning, but can have a strongly favorable impact on your income—business and personal. Keep in mind, however, that leverage of any kind is always a double-edged sword. The same mathematics that will magnify your profits when you are operating above the break-even point, will cause accelerated losses when your sales fall below the break-even point. Knowing what these numbers are, and being able to tweak the variables that control them, is obviously crucial to prudent management and the prudent use of leverage.

You now have an understanding of the impact that relatively few variables (price, quantity, variable costs and fixed costs) can have on your bottom line, and why you should manage them carefully. But before you begin to determine how many units or hours you need to sell to cover all of your costs, I'd like to take you back to a point earlier in this chapter where I said an owner wanted to earn $2,500 "excess cash."

The Way It Should Be

Where did the number $2,500 come from? What does that number represent? Is it the "right number?" These and other questions should come to mind when establishing your sales goals, and this is another area where the textbook approach to break-even analysis goes lacking. In order to grow your business (and some level of growth is essential even for those who want merely to establish a modest "lifestyle" business), you must budget for some level of retained earnings. Retained earnings, while not to be confused with cash, represent the amount of past profits that you have set aside to reinvest in the future of your business and to fund its growth. Retained earnings are especially crucial if, whether by choice or force, you have little or no debt.

In other words, in addition to just breaking even, you must budget for a profit. How much profit will depend on your industry, your company and your own personal goals and ambitions. If that number for the owner of our software company was $2,500 a month ($30,000 a year) then the owner should add that amount to the total "fixed costs" that must be covered.

Assuming no increase in prices, this means the break-even point has been increased by about 32 units a month. Don't fear a higher sales number, or be overly conservative by a misguided desire to "break even." The next step in this book will make achieving such increases ridiculously easy, and besides, why in the world would you want to set sales targets that ensure your business will never have enough money to grow? And retained earnings is not all that we should add to the "fixed cost" nut. For planning purposes (not necessarily what you would show to your banker), now is the time to add in *all* of the overhead expenses that would be present if this were the business you dreamed of running, rather than the one you are currently running. If you're operating out of your kitchen, but would like to have that executive suite around the corner for $800 a month, bundle that $9,600 a year number into your fixed costs to see how many units you need to sell to get there. Break-even analysis is not just a financial report; it's primarily a goal setting and planning tool. Use it that way.

If you're paying yourself $2,000 a month, but you know that number should be $5,000, then bundle the $36,000 a year difference into fixed costs to set some *exciting* goals for sales, not survival goals. (More about this in Step 7, but it is proven that *challenging* goals are the most effective.)

And one more thing: What are you going to retire on? Or, even before you retire, are there certain lifestyle rewards that you want such as cars, second homes or world travel? Well, if so, and if they exceed what can be paid for out of your wages, then you had better bundle them into your "what if?" analysis as well.

But let's go back to our software company owner and let's keep our assumptions that he currently has fixed costs of $240,000 a year, which was originally the sole number in the numerator of his break-even formula. (Actually, we used $20,000 per month.) Budgeting for retained earnings of $30,000, he needs to increase the numerator to $270,000, which requires selling 3,417 units at $89, or about 285 units a month—32 more than the original break-even point, but an amount that will keep the business growing.

Paying For The Dream

Up to this point, we've more or less looked at the existing business model for this software company and tried to tweak it. Now, let's work backwards from a big personal goal, and see if this business can handle the load. Suppose that we've gone to the owner of ABC and asked if he would like to retire. His answer is "*Yes!*" He tells us that he is willing to work for fifteen more years and, though his primary home will be paid off by then, he wants a second home in Santa Fe that will cost around $750,000. In addition, he wants to travel, drive a nice car, have some life insurance, give to worthy causes and do a few other things. He could consult or even run a small business on the side, but for safety's sake, he says we had best plan for no outside sources of income. He wants to be able to live on his savings.

And how much does he have in savings now?

About the same amount as most small business owners. You know...zero! Oh, maybe there's a retirement plan somewhere, or some stocks, but the capital intensive nature of small businesses, combined with the lack of available capital, almost guarantees that small business owners will find it next to impossible to save while they own their businesses. Which is why many believe, or want to believe, that they are building up equity in their businesses, and that their retirement nest egg will come from the sale of that business. But, as I pointed out earlier, this is often the road to disappointment and should be avoided at all costs. If your business sells, let that be the icing on the cake, but please plan your life around factors that you can control. It's your life!

Our software owner agrees with this and assumes that because he is such a vital part of his business, when he retires, his company will simply close its doors. It will provide no further income for him. The next step then, is for him to figure out how much money he needs to save to fund his chosen retirement lifestyle. This calculation can be as simple or as complex as an individual desires. There are dozens of great calculators on various Web sites that will walk you through 15-20 minutes of detailed questions (including life expectancy, tax rate, Social Security, retirement plans, etc.) and provide you with The Answer. Most of the major brokerage firms offer such calculators, or you can just do an Internet search for financial calculators. I encourage you to explore for and find one that works for you.

Since this book is not intended to teach you about compound interest and net present value, however, I'm going to take a more simplistic approach. I'm going to say that our software company owner has determined that he wants to pay cash for his second home (he will not have a mortgage payment on either house), and therefore can live comfortably on $100,000 a year. To be ultra-conservative, he's not going to worry about life expectancy because he doesn't want to risk *any* principal—he'll just leave it to his children. This means the $100,000 a year must be a safe, relatively low return on some principal amount. The question is, what's that amount?

Perhaps the easiest way to calculate this amount is to capitalize the $100,000 income stream by dividing it by the required rate of return. Forgetting tax-free versus taxable rates for now, let's just assume a 7% rate of return. Dividing $100,000 by .07 derives a number just over $1.4 million. Get it? A lump sum of $1.4 million earning 7% interest will throw off $100,000 cash each year...forever!

So, he needs $1.4 million, plus the $750,000 to pay for his Santa Fe house, or a total of $2.15 million, which I'll call $2.2 million in the interest of rounding conservatively.

I hope the next obvious question is leaping to the front of your mind. How much does he need to take out of his business each of the next fifteen years, in order to end up with $2.2 million? Whatever that annual number is, it also needs to be added to the other "fixed costs" in his break-out analysis, in order to see how many units he really, *really* needs to sell in order to grow his business and fund his lifestyle goals. Isn't that what entrepreneurship is supposed to be about?

To find out what annual or monthly contribution will result in $2.2 million over 15 years at a given rate of return, you *will* need a financial calculator—either the hand-held type or one from a Web site. (At least I do!) But I'll solve this one for you, and you might be surprised. To have his home in Santa Fe and his six-figure income for the rest of his natural days, our software company owner needs to put aside only about $4,000 a month. I admit that's assuming a healthy 15% rate of return, but it's also starting from zero savings now!

Using your break-even tools, you can quickly discern that he will have to increase sales by about 51 units a month, or;

$20,000 + $4,000 = $24,000
$24,000 / $79 = 304 units
304 units - 253 units = 51 units

And if prices were increased? If variable costs were slashed? If fixed costs were trimmed? Learn to play with the numbers until you see a formula—a strategy—that you like and feel confident can be achieved.

The next step, Step 7, will show you more about how to create the details of the plan necessary to accomplish this, but the point I want to make here is that what first appeared to be a huge lifetime goal—millions of dollars—can often be easily reached. All you have to do is get very specific on what you want, do the math and start to work.

Photo Map Update

The sixth area of consideration for your photo map is what I term spiritualism. For some, this may be a strict, organized religion, while for others it may be a self-discovered form of meditation and thoughtfulness. The point is that our businesses and lives can become so complex that it is essential to have a source of strength that is greater than ourselves, something to put our day-to-day concerns in perspective. For me, sometimes just starting a program of reading about different spiritual philosophies is very comforting. Even ten minutes in the evening will do. I also like to take long walking meditations—sometimes with a tape recorder in hand. While it is possible for our mind to hold dozens of competing thoughts at one time, it is possible to speak about only one at a time.

For some, a photographic image of spiritualism may range from a traditional religious leader, to a sunset, to a scene of nature and the world at work. Whatever you choose, make sure that when you view it, you feel an immediate, if slight, wave of comfort and confidence envelop you. This image should remind you that there is even more to life than all the things we have depicted through our photo maps.

Reducing To The Ridiculous

Step 7

A journey of a thousand miles begins with a single step.

—Lao-tzu

The art of reducing something to the ridiculous, a term I have borrowed from sales guru Tom Hopkins, is nothing more than breaking big goals down into bite-sized pieces. The difference between desire and reality is called frustration, and when we set big goals (which I encourage) we may be intimidated by how far away from them we feel. When there is no clear path toward the big goal, when the distance from where we are to where we want to be seems too great, our natural inclination is to do...nothing. But when big goals are broken down into daily activities, we begin to make progress that creates a sense of momentum that builds upon itself. I can't write a *New York Times* bestseller today, but I can write a darn good paragraph if I will just work on it. Writing one good paragraph each day for a period of two or three years yields a good book. Whether it becomes a *New York Times* bestseller may be beyond my control, but whether or not it gets written in the first place is directly and solely under my control. And, the chances of hitting that bestseller list are greatly improved if I've actually written a book, wouldn't you agree? Now, how does this step-by-step philosophy apply to your goals?

One thing that graduates of 8-steps workshops often mention is the fact that lifetime goals they had given up on, or which previously seemed too high to even consider, suddenly seem within reach again. For example, after ten tough years in business, the owner of a fire safety company woke up to the fact that he didn't have any real savings, and was no longer optimistic that he could sell his business for enough to retire on. He told me that he didn't mind working for an additional ten years, but that he had always hoped to end up with a million dollars to sustain his lifestyle. Based on past experience, he now didn't see any way he could save that amount. I could feel his onrushing sense of panic tinged with self-disappointment.

First, I reminded him that it didn't matter where he was today (there's nothing anyone can do about that), only which direction he was heading—and that can be changed in an instant. Second, I reminded him that in creating a business, he had created a model that was capable of generating excess cash, if it was properly tuned. That he had managed to survive was proof positive that he could thrive. I also told him that once he had a clear goal, the daily commitment required to achieve that goal might actually be quite small—like writing a book one paragraph at a time. He could achieve his million-dollar savings goal, I assured him, but he was skeptical, so I walked him through this seventh step.

Assuming that he was certain that $1 million was the right number, he needed to determine how much he would have to save each year in order to meet that goal. Once that savings number was known, we could modify his business model to generate the necessary "excess cash." If there was no way his present business could support those objectives, he could at least face the truth and either change his long-term goals or change his business. By using a Web-based financial calculator available at most bank, brokerage and insurance Web sites, he discovered that his million-dollar goal would take a savings of about $60,000 per year for the next ten years. That is the amount of "excess cash," then, that we needed to retool his company to generate, an amount that would double his pervious earnings on annual sales of $1 million. Again, there are significant tax issues here that I am avoiding for the sake of simplicity, but which you should discuss with your CPA.

Now, knowing what you do about the 8 steps, I bet you can think of lots of ways that the owner of this company could increase profits and start saving toward his million-dollar goal. Not least among them, he should definitely try to sell up, not out....that is, to sell more to his existing customers. He should also increase his switching costs and raise his prices. It would, after all, take only a 6% increase in prices to achieve *all* of his savings goals with no extra effort. (A 6% price increase on annual sales of $1 million would add $60,000 to the top—*and bottom*—lines.)

Constructing A Personal Dashboard

But for this example, I want to tackle the worst case. Here, in order to double earnings, we really are going to double sales *volume*, even if it means doubling the customer base and the complexity of the company. What I'm most interested in is discovering which activities we can regularly measure that are most likely to lead us to that doubling of sales volume. I'm not willing to wait ten years and then determine whether he was successful. I want something that I can measure monthly, weekly...even daily that will guarantee he meets his long-term goals.

At the heart of this crucial seventh step, is the creation of a system of measures—a dashboard—that will keep you on track toward your goals, and the reduction of those measures to small increments that are easily attainable in the short term. As Ray Kroc, the force behind McDonald's said, "Nothing is particularly hard if broken down into small parts." That includes paying for your dreams.

We track, or measure, these small increments because even after your "car" is on the right road, you'll still want to monitor speed, engine temperature, fuel, etc., on a regular basis to make sure you arrive safely at your final destiny...I mean, destination. Your dashboard will be unique to your business. It will not necessarily contain traditional measures such as profitability or financial ratios. Rather, your dashboard measures will largely be the result of your creativity and your deep, personal understanding of what *really* makes your business tick.

In the case of the fire safety company, I suspected that a sales efficiency measure could be valuable. Though it's just one of many you might create for your firm, I've often had success with this measure, regardless of the nature of the business. The crucial measures for sales efficiency relate to *pre-sales* activities. To put it simply, I worked backwards from the point of sale to see exactly what the steps were that led up to a sale. Since we're assuming in this case that we must double sales volume, these measures focused on new sales rather than on repeat sales. In general, here is the sales process that I discovered:

- A prospect list is compiled or purchased;
- A phone call is made to set an appointment;
- An appointment is made to make a presentation of capability;
- A proposal is delivered with specifications and pricing;
- A contract is signed and an average sale of $10,000 is made.

With sales of about $1 million in the most recent year, and an average sale of $10,000, we can assume they sell to 100 customers—50 each for the two sales representatives. Based on this level of sales, the owner was managing to keep the company going, and taking about $60,000 a year out for himself.

In other words, he needed to precisely double his discretionary income in order to meet his long-term savings goal.

When looking for a sales efficiency measure, what I'm most interested in are the *ratios* of one activity to the one that follows it. For example, how many phone calls does it take, on average, to get an appointment? Two? Five? Twenty-five? And how many appointments lead to a proposal? And, ultimately, how many proposals result in a sale? Every company should know these vital sales efficiency measures. In this case, the ratios were as follows:

Sales cycle	Ratios	Cumulative
A list is obtained	N/A	N/A
A phone call is made to set an appointment	N/A	N/A
A presentation is made	10 to 1	10 to 1
A proposal is delivered	2 to 1	20 to 1
A sale is made	5 to 1	100 to 1

The first two steps are designated "not applicable" because no ratios apply. The number of prospects on our list is our beginning point and there is nothing to prevent 100% of those names from being called. However, once we start calling decision-makers by phone, history tells us that we are given the chance to make a presentation to only one out of ten. This takes into account bad numbers on our list, companies that are now defunct and people who simply will not accept our phone calls or refuse to set an appointment.

After a presentation is made to the one out of ten we initially called, we find that one out of two asks for a complete proposal, and of those who receive proposals, one out of five become customers. Multiplying these ratios together (as shown on the chart above), we discover that out of all the names on our original list, one in 100 will become customers, each with an average sale of $10,000.

But the question remains, how do we double sales? Assuming this company has been around for a few years, it would lack credibility if the owner went to his sales representatives and simply announced a doubling of sales as the goal with no other changes. But, what if he asked his sales representatives to make an extra phone call or two each hour? How hard would that be? What would the impact be? Would it be enough? Let's see what the sales efficiency ratios say.

Based on the current ratios, to gain 100 new customers the two sales representatives would have to collectively contact 10,000 new prospects within the next year. Does that sound like a lot? We'll, let's see. Ten thousand prospects at the given ratios, means 10,000 phone calls, 1,000 presentations, 500 proposals and 100 sales. Given that there are two sales reps, that's 5,000 phone calls, 500 presentations, 250 proposals and 50 sales for each.

Does this still seem like a lot of activity? Let's reduce these numbers to the ridiculous. Five thousand phone calls in 50 weeks (we'll give them two weeks of vacation) is 100 a week. That's 20 a day. That's 2.5 an hour. And since 90% of the phone calls will be very short (less than a minute, I would venture) that's not too demanding for a full-time professional salesperson—probably less than five minutes.

Continuing this logic, 500 presentations is ten a week or two a day. Two-hundred-fifty proposals is five a week, or one a day. And 50 sales is one a week. What results is the profile of a salesperson who comes in at 8:00 a.m., makes 20 prospecting calls before 9:00 a.m., prints and mails out one proposal before 10:00 a.m., and then prepares for two presentations that day. Granted, this is in addition to their current level of activity, but tending to existing business often takes far less time than finding new customers. Oh yes, let's not forget that one day during the week they'll also pick up an order. Not exactly slave labor.

So yes, in this case asking his sales people to make one or two more calls per hour *would* make the difference between this owner surviving or thriving. The difference between this owner's state of frustration and his desired lifestyle for the future was a very small change in day-to-day activities. When reduced to the ridiculous, a big goal was turned into easily achievable daily tasks.

Again, keep in mind that this example is extremely conservative. It is inconceivable that the owner, through applying the other steps in this book, would actually have to *double* his customer base in order to double earnings. More likely, these added calls would lead to an even greater bottom line impact—he may very well meet his million-dollar savings goal well ahead of schedule.

Beating Pete Sampras

If you're a sedentary couch potato, but have a goal of running a marathon, you don't enter one that weekend, do you? More likely, you'll walk a mile. Then you'll walk two. Then you'll jog a mile. Then you'll jog two...then five...then ten...and maybe a year, or six years from now, you'll be ready to complete the 26.2 mile marathon. You don't pick up a golf club for the first time and say, "Bring on Tiger Woods." You don't take your first piano lesson and play Mozart. Everything that we successfully do is broken down into small parts, and talent is only part of the equation. Can you beat Pete Sampras in tennis? Of course you can't. Could you beat him if he had never picked up a racket and you had practiced four hours a day for your entire life? Of course you could. The "talent" is the same in both cases, but the victor is determined based on practice—one day at a time. One paragraph at a time. One sales call at a time. Creating the proper measures is your way to practice success in business.

If you work for McDonald's, successful practice would be broken down for you through extensive training. If you take piano lessons, the lesson books have broken the key elements of practice down for you. (Notes, scales, chords, etc.) But no one has ever broken down your business or your lifetime goals into manageable increments for you and your employees to practice. And no one except for you ever will because those increments—your dashboard—are unique to your business and unique to your life. No one can or will discover them for you. You must discover them for yourself.

Think about that. I'm telling you that there are precious few, but critical things that you must measure in order to achieve all of your business and personal goals. Then, I'm telling you that I can't tell you what those things are! But they are worth searching for, because when you find them, everything you do will suddenly matter.

What Gets Measured Gets Done

I used to fly a small airplane as a hobby—a Cessna 172. The instrument panel of this plane is wonderfully simple. There is an oil pressure and fuel gauge, an altimeter and air speed indicator, a compass...and little else. Those crucial gauges are all that are really necessary to fly that plane. Then one day, I was walking through a gift store in a local mall and noticed a large poster of the cockpit of a Boeing 747. I was stunned! There were hundreds of gauges, dials and buttons all over the place—literally above, below, in front of and to all sides of the pilots. It was hard for me to imagine how anyone could monitor that many measurements.

And then a funny thing happened. As I stared at the poster, my eyes zeroed in on the area of the instrument panel directly in front of the pilot, just beyond the control yoke. Guess what I saw? An altimeter, an airspeed indicator, a compass...the same instruments in almost the same place that my tiny single-engine plane contained. I thought of Pareto, and it occurred to me that even those highly skilled pilots probably spend 80% of their time monitoring the same gauges I did when flying my little plane. No matter what the size or the complexity of the machine, there are only a precious few instruments that are truly vital. The rest are just luxuries and you don't have the resources to monitor luxuries!

The good news, then, is that you only need to monitor a few crucial gauges. The bad news, as I mentioned above, is that, unlike airplanes, every small business will have *different* gauges, and your most important tasks will be to identify those four or five measures that will not only demonstrate your improvement, but will predict your future success.

This forward-looking approach to tracking a business is new—even by *Fortune* 500 standards. One example of its popularity is evidenced by the success of the book *The Balanced Scorecard,* written by David P. Norton and Robert S. Kaplan. While this book would probably not make Pareto's reading list for small business owners, it is very popular within large firms and in academic circles. In general, it promotes development of a unique "scorecard" that contains leading indicators that can predict the successful implementation of strategy. Norton and Kaplan speak of developing a system of measures that can "tell the story" of a firm. I like that.

The Balanced Scorecard approach seeks to link measures from crucial areas inside *and outside* of the company. The four areas from which measures are to be created are:

- Customer Perspective (How do our customers see us?)
- Internal Perspective (What must we excel at?)
- Innovation and Learning (How can we continue to improve?)
- Financial Perspective (How do we look to our owners?)

What Kaplan and Norton mean by "telling the story" of the firm is that key measures in each of these areas are linked to those in other areas. Suppose, for example, that in the previous case we have determined that the number of telephone prospecting calls a day is crucial for our future success. (Note that we are using today's calls as a *leading* indicator of future success.) Since we must have a competitive product to sell when our sales reps are on the phone, we further decide to create the most dependable (lowest failure rate) fire extinguishers on the market; this becomes our driving competitive position, our central point of uniqueness.

A Balanced Scorecard for this fire safety company might appear as follows:

• Customer Perspective—our customers will see us as providing the premiere product on the market, which, even if more expensive, protects them against not only fire, but also potential lawsuits. We will achieve a defect rate of less than .01% to be determined by tracking every attempted customer discharge of fire extinguishers. We will survey our customers annually to ensure that we are rated at the top of the quality charts.

• Internal Perspective—we must excel at manufacturing reliable, high-quality fire safety devices, and at selling them. We will have goals and measures for both areas. For sales, our goal is to increase the number of weekly prospecting calls by 100. We will develop a poster-sized graph of our call rate that will be prominently displayed in the sales area. If the additional prospecting calls for the week have been completed by 2:00 p.m. on Friday, the sales representatives are free to leave for the weekend.

• Innovation and Learning—to facilitate this increased sales call level, we will install a computerized contact management system and provide the sales reps with training and other efficiency aids such as telephone headsets. This contact management system will also generate the necessary letters and automate the proposal process. Sales reps will be able to make more contacts in less time than before. This will be measured by total time spent on administrative work versus total dollar volume of orders. We want to see that ratio decline by 10% a year for the next three years.

• Financial Perspective—our improved sales efficiency and commitment to product quality will increase sales 100% and maintain gross profit margins, doubling net earnings. This can be measured by traditional financial statements and ratios. We will seek to increase leverage each year, so that earnings increase at a faster rate than sales.

Do you see how these measures and their associated goals "tell the story" of this business? I suggest that you brainstorm many different measures and corresponding goals, but that you actually create your dashboard, or instrument panel, using no more than 3 in each of the above areas, for a total of twelve. Even that may be too many—pick four that you consider especially critical. Properly constructed, these gauges have the effect of automatically reducing big goals to manageable parts. And celebrate your wins—large and small—as often as possible. Build the sense of momentum. Tie specific rewards (like leaving at 2:00 p.m. on Fridays) to the accomplishment of the activities that will lead you to your greatest goals.

Another related term frequently used in consulting is "key success factors," often shortened to KSF. That is what these "balanced" measures are trying to reveal: What are the key success factors for your firm? You must spend time exposing the candidates and selecting the winners in terms of what is crucial to your company. You must admit that you cannot do it all, and use these measures to help you focus on that which you absolutely, positively *must* do and do well! Then, you must monitor your dashboard gauges vigilantly.

A bank wanting to change its image from passive (offering mostly CDs and checking accounts) to aggressive (money management, brokerage services, etc.) retrained its officers, and began measuring how much time they spent face-to-face with customers. Think about it. It doesn't take long to tell a customer what a CD is yielding, but it takes quite a while to explain mutual funds, 401(k) plans, etc. Unless they were talking about the weather, more time spent with customers was an excellent leading indicator for the sale of new products.

A company whose key success factor is continual innovation might choose to measure sales from new products as a percentage of total sales. Or, they could measure R&D expenditures. Or, they could measure their investment in continuing education for their key personnel. A company emphasizing personal customer service might set a goal of reducing staff turnover, which could be easily measured and could lead to specific actions to improve that number.

Stop right now and write down four KSFs for your firm. These may change as you work your way through the 8 steps, but first impressions are often very important.

More On Setting Goals

As I've previously mentioned, I'm not attempting to write a book on goal setting, but I would like to share a few factors that have proven successful in this regard. These will work both with your large lifetime goals, and your daily "balanced scorecard" goals.

• Goals must be big enough to matter. I've talked a lot about "big goals," but once again let me remind you that your photo map and other long-term goals need to be challenging. Studies have found that specific *difficult* goals, so long as they are not absurd, are the most motivating.

• Goals must be written down and either left on display, or reviewed frequently. A photo map is the ultimate manifestation of this.

• Goals are more powerful if they can be made visual, such as those in your photo map.

• Goals must have a timeline for accomplishment.

• Goals should be stated in the positive, not the negative. For example, you should state your goals like this: "I will have a beautiful second home in the wine country within five years so that I may paint and teach others to paint." You should *not* say, "If I don't have a second home in the wine country within five years it will prove that I'll never amount to anything and that I'm not good enough to help others learn to paint."

• Goals should be shared. I have to admit, I've battled this one over time and it may be a simple matter of personal preference. I have read experts who advise sharing goals, and experts who advise *never* telling anyone your goals for fear of a cool, demoralizing reaction. I've tried both approaches, but what works best for me is to openly announce the goal (no matter how outlandish it may seem to others), but keep the specifics of how I'm going to accomplish that goal to myself. Usually the "how" is too detailed to explain to casual friends anyway. When pressed, I'll respond in a very vague or general manner, even if I have a detailed written plan. It's almost like having an intriguing secret that others can tell you are keeping from them.

- Goals should be supported by as many reasons as possible about why that goal will benefit as many people as possible.
- If the goal itself is not a reward, the goal should have a reward attached to it. Great health, for example, is hard to quantify. If I used the completion of a marathon as a fitness goal, I might attach a trip to Cancun as my reward. I believe strongly in being nice to yourself, whether it is getting regular massages, taking extra days off, traveling or just consciously attaching tangible rewards to the many accomplishments we seldom take note of.
- List specific actions that you can take on a daily basis that will move you toward your goal, rank these actions in order of their contribution and start working on the most important. Revisit and update this list weekly. Celebrate the small wins that are leading you toward your big dreams.

That's really all there is to it. Of course, once you see this process working in your life, you may want to offer it to your employees as well. Encourage them to set goals that link *their* personal ambitions to the goals of your organization. Like most people, they'll ultimately work harder for themselves than they will for you. Why not harness that effort for the best results for both?

Photo Map Update

The seventh area of consideration for your photo map is to find an image that represents financial security to you. As described in the Introduction, you may want to select an obscure image (a landscape, for example) but then tell yourself the "story" of how that picture implies that you have "made it." In this case, it may be that the view of the landscape as seen from the balcony of your retirement villa, or perhaps is part of the vineyard you acquired after leaving your small business behind.

Others may prefer more obvious signs of wealth such as private jets, yachts, luxury cars, etc. And still others may want to add the personal touch by including children in cap and gowns, older parents in comfortable settings, etc.

Use whatever works for you, but please remember that dreams cost money. Take the powerful step of actually estimating what your dreams will cost. I don't care if you don't have a nickel to your name, if you want a yacht as part of your retirement, pick up the phone or go online, and find out how much the yacht you want costs. Then, using the logic presented in this chapter, determine what your business model must contribute, and for how long, in order to make that dream a reality. Then, put that yacht on your photo map and look at it every day as you start working on the small actions that will consistently and positively lead to its attainment.

Happy sailing.

Adjusting All Your Means

First have a definite, clear, practical ideal—a goal. Second, have the necessary means to achieve your ends—wisdom, money, materials and methods. Third, adjust all your means to that end.

—Aristotle

Many years ago, before I had become an entrepreneur on my own, I managed 65 employees in eighteen sales offices for a new division of a large company. The only problem was, we had no sales!

As the sales manager, I worried more than a little about my job security. But George More, CEO of this high-tech startup and my boss, did not seem concerned that our pricey computer graphics systems were not selling. Despite our dismal results, we had strong financial backing, and for almost a year, George told me to keep hiring, training and managing salespeople, to staff those eighteen quiet offices.

Even so, after more months passed without a single sale, I finally went to George to express the depth of my concern over morale and to propose sales incentives. Again, George told me not to worry. He told me to leave it to him.

A few days later when I arrived at work, I was stunned to find an enormous brass bell in the midst of our cubicles.

The bell, easily three feet in circumference, was mounted in a sturdy wooden frame that stood six feet tall. The Queen Mary would have been proud of this bell. Later in the day, our curiosity piqued, George called a meeting near the bell and informed us that Liz, our customer support manager (though we had no customers) was hereby ordered to ring the bell as loudly as she could whenever orders were received. *Orders*?

From that day on, the bell became the object of our constant attention. People touched it, rubbed it for good luck, pretended to ring it, talked about it and joked about it. One day it was polished, the next day a mustache was affixed to it and soon it sported a wig. The only thing it didn't do was ring. Day after day it just hung there, quiet as the phones in customer support. Week after week.

And then one afternoon, an explosive sound, as disconcerting as a smoke alarm in the middle of the night. *DING, DONG, DING, DONG!* Louder than anyone, including George, could ever have imagined. Even as we covered our ears, employees from all departments charged out of their cubicles and stampeded toward the bell. Who had made the sale? In which city? To whom? When would we ship? High fives. *Yeah!*

After that first time, no one could walk by the bell without casting a wary eye. Was the next deafening ring imminent? To whom was Liz talking on the phone? People from every department called the individual sales representatives, putting pressure on them. "Get with it, you guys. We want to hear the bell again!" And three weeks later we did. DING, DONG, DING, DONG! And again two weeks later. Suddenly, after having suffered through months with no sales, three sales in five weeks created a fever pitch of optimism that bordered on cockiness, not to mention a healthy competition among the sales representatives.

You Are What You Think

Although the bell had rung only three times, it now *seemed* as if it was ringing constantly. Like the news media giving extensive coverage to uncommon events until they seem common, George More, a creative genius, had made the rare seem commonplace. He had mentally set up his employees to anticipate and celebrate only the good news—the bell. With amazing speed, employees changed their focus from counting the days of our ineptitude to imagining a dynamic future. The entire organization radiated enthusiasm and raced to $20 million in sales! We were soon making so many sales that we had to reduce the bell-ringing to a single DING, because it was becoming too distracting. But this method of drawing attention to our wins had certainly been a ringing success.

I mentioned that George More had "set" his employees up to constantly anticipate the bell, though it rarely rang. This concept of "set" is a powerful and proven psychological principle that can have the same positive effect on your business that it had on George More's. It is also one of the most powerful tools available to link business strategy to achieving personal lifetime goals. Here's how it works, with or without a bell: People see, hear and experience what they *expect* to see, hear and experience. Our interpretation of events is adjusted to neatly fit that set of expectations. This principle has been written about for thousands of years by the some of the greatest minds in history. "We become what we think about all day long," said Ralph Waldo Emerson. Perhaps cursed with a writer's ego, he may have felt compelled to embellish Buddha ("We are what we think.") and Proverbs 23:7 ("As he thinketh in his heart, so is he.") All of them express a fact of human existence that can be proven by faith *or* science.

In *The Brain Book*, Peter Russell defines this long-proven phenomenon as, "any belief system will make a person 'set' to notice those events and facts that support their belief and miss those that do not." Mark Brown, author of *Why Dogs Look Like Their Owners*, points out that if we see a fat man with a pug nose walking a fat dog with a pug nose, we will laugh about how dog and man look alike. We have "set" ourselves to notice the few similarities, ignoring the facts that only one of them has fur, four legs and a tail, that in truth, they look nothing at all alike.

An extreme example of set can be observed following tragedies when people often fall back on their religious beliefs. Survivors of natural disasters are often quick to give "thanks" to God despite the fact that, for example, a tornado has just destroyed their home and killed several neighbors. Rather than question the same God who has presumably wrought the destruction, they focus on their own survival, reaffirming their chosen belief system. Paradoxically, their faith is strengthened as a result of a disaster sent their way.

Seeing only that which reaffirms our beliefs, we create an enormous sense of momentum. The bell seems to ring more often than it actually does. Future rings seem imminent, inevitable. We truly do become what we focus on. Can you see why setting up and measuring small, incremental goals—and celebrating them—can lead to such positive long-term results? More than half the battle is just being clear about that which we highlight. In a typical day, phone calls, e-mails, faxes and other activities can overwhelm us. If there are no clear priorities for the business, we respond in the order of their occurrence rather than the order of their importance. The day can seem chaotic yet trivial. But, if we respond in order of relevance to our long-term goals (the photo map for those using it), our progress becomes obvious, our optimism becomes contagious and we are reminded that there are few greater mysteries in life than the scientific fact that if we believe we are getting better, *we are!*

Time is your greatest asset. Your only asset, really. Where and how you spend your time will determine the success of your business and your life. How could it be any other way? As I noted in the Introduction, for my entire adult life, when asked what I really wanted to do, I would answer, "write." The only problem was, I wasn't doing any writing. I didn't have time. I was too busy doing what everyone else wanted me to do, and what I believed I was committed to do for financial security.

So, was I becoming a better writer? Was I learning what was necessary to succeed? Of course not! To do more of what mattered to me, I needed to do less of all those other things. I needed to make some difficult changes and take some uncomfortable risks. While I have advocated throughout this book the importance of small changes, there may also come a time for major ones.

Practice Being You

When I made time for writing, I learned. I practiced. I studied. And with two books written now, I'm getting better. But, before I could tackle what was important to me, I had to make room for *new* tasks. If a bathtub is full, but too cool for your liking, you've got to let some cold water out before you can put hot water in. Today, everyone's tub is full, so before we can add we must subtract. We've got to do less, thereby enabling us to do more of what *matters*!

Williams Jennings Bryan said, "Destiny is not a matter of chance, it's a matter of choice." Since the choices you make will determine your destiny, you must first choose how to spend your time.

Now that you have streamlined your business model and focused your time on the priorities that matter most, it is a relatively simple thing to expand your business without recreating the chaos and inefficiencies that you have left behind. A business owner must be many things—salesman, buyer, manager, accountant, janitor and file clerk, to name a few. But no activity the business owner can undertake affects success like the development of strategy. Amar Bhidi, former Associate Professor at The Harvard Business School, said it this way: "Ventures based on a great strategy can survive confusion and poor leadership, but sophisticated control systems and organizational structures cannot compensate for an unsound strategy." In other words, we can succeed in spite of ourselves if our strategy is good, and under almost no circumstances if it is flawed.

A good strategy is largely the result of focusing on a few key success factors that drive your business—the things that *really* matter. A good strategy does not try to be all things to all people, but seeks to empty your container of fruitless busy work, and fill it with highly focused goal-directed activities. Hopefully, the 8 steps have already helped you to identify these activities.

Nor is developing a strategy a complicated process. Simply stated, a strategy is a method of doing something; in this case, a method of achieving certain goals—business and personal. I would rather you devote six minutes to strategy than six months. I would rather you write it on the back of a napkin than on a hundred pages of pretty paper. A good strategy is always simple, straightforward and inspired.

When we have linked our business activities to our lifetime goals, strategy becomes the method for achieving both. Michael Porter of The Harvard Business School is a master of business strategy. For years, I have been using his concepts both in the classroom and in the real world. Porter maintains that there are only three strategies available to any firm, large or small. The three are:

- Overall cost leadership
- Differentiation
- Focus

As mentioned earlier, overall cost leadership requires access to large amounts of capital, intensive control systems and management depth, so it is not available to most small firms. If you think you're a cost leader, you're probably confusing cost with price.

Having eliminated overall cost leadership as a strategy, we are left with focus and differentiation. You'll use both. First, you'll focus on a group of customers with shared characteristics—those that "look like" your Ideal Customers, though they will have slightly different "personalities." Then, using many of the 8 steps, you will differentiate your products and services within that segment to create uniqueness in your customers' minds. It's that simple and here's how it works in practice.

Some years ago, I became involved a small company (roughly $1 million in annual sales with twelve employees) that described itself as a data processing firm. With revenues essentially flat for years, the three owners were looking for some ideas to get unstuck.

The first part of the process, as described in Step 2, was to find out where the company was making money and where it was losing money. That is, to do less and make more. Remember, even microbusinesses evolve over the years into many segments because of their inability to say "No." All systems tend toward disorder. Just as your garage and desk drawers get messy without your constant attention, so does your business. In this case, revenue was being derived from sources as diverse as computer hardware sales, data processing services, and payroll services to both large and small customers.

To stop losing money, the company took my advice and got out of the hardware business. Then, with more room in their container for other things, the next step was to determine what to do *more of*. We began with an analysis of the top 20% of their existing customers. Applying Pareto's Law it is common that examining the top 20% of customers will encompass close to 80% of the firm's total revenues. I discovered that the greatest need of their best customers was not just for data processing, but for *payroll* processing.

Before making any more recommendations, I wanted to understand the payroll services industry and identify those competitors that could provide the same goods or services. I began to brainstorm how my client might separate itself from the pack. I started by researching large public companies that do data processing. Even though there are important differences between public and private companies, there are also similarities, and, since public companies must disclose vast amounts of information, it is remarkably easy to find out their secrets. (Check online or at your library for annual reports, 10Ks and other documents regularly produced by public companies, as well as independent reports by the analysts who follow them.) With the resources available today, we're not talking about an investment of months, but of hours. The return is more than worth it.

Outfocusing The Focuser

What I discovered was that in the 1960s, IBM had dominated the payroll processing business. However, since IBM also dominated every other area of data processing, payroll constituted only a tiny sliver of its overall revenue. The company's sales personnel were neither highly focused on, nor trained in, the complexities of payroll. No doubt, some customers received services and reports they liked, while others had to take what they could get.

Then, in the 1970s, a small payroll and bookkeeping firm called ADP was looking for growth opportunities. I suspect that somewhere in their early stages, management thinking went like this:

> *The portion of IBM's revenue that comes from payroll processing is tiny to IBM, but would be huge to us. If we do nothing but process payroll, our sales and customer support people will be experts, our software can be optimized and our reports can be customized. We will simply produce a better product than IBM even though they are many times larger. And, since we will call only on human resource managers, our sales effort will be much more efficient than IBM's, perhaps even allowing us to outspend IBM on that small portion of their total market.*

The strategy worked. By outfocusing IBM, ADP became a very successful company that today registers over $5 billion in sales. Which is big enough to encourage even more focused competitors to find a vulnerable sliver of ADP's pie. So, when a company called Paychex started out in Rochester, New York, I suspect their thought process went something like this:

> *ADP has become very successful and is growing rapidly by outfocusing IBM in the payroll processing market. But maybe in concentrating on the* Fortune *500, there are segments of the market that ADP is overlooking. Maybe there is a small slice of ADP's pie that would make a nice company for us.*

And Paychex discovered that niche in servicing the unique needs of *small* businesses. By outfocusing the focuser again, Paychex built a very nice, profitable business that today boasts annual sales of over $1 billion.

The information uncovered about Paychex warmed our hearts with the knowledge that payroll services were a growing and profitable business. But we knew that to succeed, to create a sustainable niche, we too needed to outfocus the focuser. So we studied the business of Paychex more carefully. We studied their pie to see which slice we might nibble away at. Our logic went something like this:

> *Paychex services small businesses, most with fewer than 100 employees and many with less than five. But not all small businesses are alike. Perhaps certain businesses have unique, or especially complex, payroll requirements. If so, we could customize reports, add services and develop expertise in a certain niche that would give us greater competency than Paychex (or ADP or IBM).*

A brainstorming process (and a trip through the yellow pages), identified business segments that fit our criteria. Temporary employment agencies, for example, have relatively large payrolls, high turnover and the need for impeccable records and tax documents. Construction firms have special needs given their reliance on subcontractors and job costing. And restaurants have high turnover and the added complexity of such unique issues as tip reporting.

My client selected restaurants. Every restaurant in the United States? No, focus is the word here. Every restaurant in Austin, Texas. If successful, it would be easy to roll out this concept statewide or nationwide in cookie-cutter fashion.

Outspending IBM

Now, let's stop for a moment and think of the marketing impact of such a commitment. Suppose we had identified 1,000 prime restaurants in Austin as its targeted prospect base, and had decided to dedicate $100,000 to a rollout marketing campaign. (Ten percent of sales would not be uncommon for even a small firm.) That means this small company could budget $100 to reach *each* of their best prospects. With Paychex targeting perhaps *15 million* small businesses nationwide, an equivalent per-prospect marketing budget for them would be $1.5 billion—more than the company's annual revenues! The same logic with different numbers would hold true for both ADP and IBM.

Do you see the power here? When you focus intensely, and really know the needs of your handpicked Ideal Customers, you can compete against anyone, large or small. You can outspend IBM on a per-prospect basis. You could send your prospects newsletters, hats or charter a plane for them. You could hold a golf tournament or bring in big-name speakers for them. You could even meet them all personally. You can do things that a giant company could never do given its large national base. IBM could, of course, retaliate in your narrow area of focus and bury you, but don't flatter yourself. The tiny piece of its pie that you're getting ready to devour is unlikely to provoke them. If they notice at all, their attitude will more likely be, "good riddance." I doubt IBM's executives, while counting up their $81 billion in sales, worry about a local twelve-person firm's next move.

This sort of focus is important for all companies. Marketing guru Al Ries wrote an entire book entitled *Focus*, though it applies mostly to large corporations. But the need to focus is even greater for small companies where it is simply not possible to pursue multiple opportunities simultaneously, and where one failed attempt could be the final attempt.

Remember Paul Caroza, owner of Run-Tex, from Step 4? He not only understands how to grow roots with his customers, but he understands strategic focus. He once told me that Run-Tex commands a 10% share of the national market for runners' shoes. Given Paul's $3.5 million in sales, I immediately challenged him, pointing out that with over 2,000 Foot Lockers and numerous other chains, the total market for running shoes was clearly more than $35 million. He shook his head and explained to me that while others focus on shoes, he focuses on runners. Not those who want to look like runners, or those who want to mow the lawn in comfortable shoes, but those who really run. Those who run four or five days a week, who run in races and who read running magazines. The Foot Locker is in the shoe business. Paul Caroza is in the runner business.

It's so simple to develop a focused strategy that I hope it becomes second nature to you. Segment your markets into smaller and smaller segments until you find a segment you can dominate. Find something you can do *better* than even the largest competitor. If you want to grow to $10 million in sales someday, don't strive for a 1% share of a billion-dollar market, strive for a 50% share of a $20 million market. The latter position is a much safer place to be. Got it? Focus on a group of customers with similar characteristics and make yourself different in their minds. Do this, and you are on the way to a supercharged strategy.

You vs. Toilet Paper

If you're concerned about whether you can differentiate your business from others, keep in mind that your business is a direct reflection of you. Unless you've been cloned, it is no more possible for someone else to have a business "just like yours" than it is for them to have a child just like yours. Every product and service can and must be differentiated in your customer's mind. One exercise you might want to try—regardless of your business—is to walk through a supermarket with one or two colleagues, asking random questions about how the differentiation of certain products might apply in your industry.

In supermarkets, we can observe the limits of differentiation as practiced by some of the best—and best-financed—companies in the world. There, you will see how great minds and lots of dollars can make brands of salt, water and toilet paper seem different. Malls also provide good lessons in focus and differentiation, presenting as they do stores that sell only candles, only lingerie, only things under a dollar, and only things that are purple. Anything can be differentiated and you *must* distinguish yourself within your focused customer segment. These factors of differentiation become a key part of the root system that you began to grow in Step 4.

Don't be a florist. Be a specialist in high-end floral arrangements delivered to hospitals. Or, tall plants maintained for office complexes. Or low-priced roses sold exclusively over the Internet. Don't be a temporary employment agency. Be a bilingual employment agency for large high-tech companies requiring UNIX programmers. Don't be a plumber. Be a specialist in plumbing renovations, or 24 hour emergencies, or apartments, or whatever it is that enables you to appear unique to your target market. You must commit to this niche strategy even though you may fear losing business from other sources. As Andrew Grove, longtime Intel CEO (and obvious engineer) says, "Put every erg into one strategy. If you die, you die, but most die because they don't commit!"

Please keep in mind that a supercharged strategy does not begin and end with marketing. Focus and uniqueness can and must apply to every area of your business. Everything from operations, to R&D, to personnel matters must become as focused as possible to support your customers. In fact, you may find that your key success factors will not come from sales and marketing. Southwest Airlines is legendary for its low prices and adored by its customers for timely arrivals and departures, but it is the company's focus on efficient *operations* that enables it to do these other things. Wal-Mart can provide low prices only because it is extremely efficient and buys in volume. What looks like a marketing strategy—low prices—is actually driven by an operational strategy. Run-Tex focuses on the logistical challenges of races as an effective and inexpensive way to achieve massive promotion.

Think of focus as a pyramid of business decisions that support the customer. In the case of Run-Tex, the pyramid includes a foundation built around facilities—a headquarters only 50 yards from the most popular running trail in Austin. It also includes hiring that focuses on serious runners who earn twice what Foot Locker employees do because they study shoes, physiology and their inventory. They know their repeat customers by name.

Paul Caroza gets great discounts because he buys large quantities of the relatively few lines he carries. His operations repeat themselves (tent sales, race registrations and even a program to supply Austin's homeless with used running shoes), which means that through experience, Run-Tex becomes more efficient and is able to exploit the learning curve.

His marketing includes over 60 races per year involving tens of thousands of runners. The result is a highly focused, well-oiled machine. I don't care if a potential competitor has the resources of Nike, it is highly unlikely they could uproot Paul Caroza and Run-Tex in Austin, Texas.

What makes your business unique? If you're not sure, ask your Ideal Customers. And if *they're* not sure, you've got work to do, for without this uniqueness, you will not be able to grow the roots that will lead to the profits, that will lead to the excess cash...that will pay for your lifetime goals!

Photo Map Update

The eighth area of consideration for your photo map is that of lifestyle. I intentionally picked a word—lifestyle—that can be loosely defined so that you can create your own personal and meaningful interpretations. The lifestyle image should not only convey the feeling that you want to have when work is an option, but should incorporate the good feelings and enthusiasm generated by all seven of the other photo map images.

For example, my lifestyle image is a beautiful house on a hill overlooking Santa Fe, New Mexico. Many people know Santa Fe to be not only a beautiful place, but a highly spiritual place as well. It is the home to many artists and its stucco architecture and deep blue skies magically influence many people. But for me, my lifestyle story encompasses far more than that.

My grandparents were frequent travelers to Santa Fe and my mother and father lived there after my father became ill in France during World War II. When we were children, my parents took my sister, my brother and me to Santa Fe often. As boys, my brother and I went to camp there. Even after his children were grown, my father still arranged for the family to meet there for special occassions.

And when we did, it was always magical to me. The conversations always seemed hopeful—as if the deep blue Santa Fe sky was the only limit for all of our dreams. It brought out the artist in all of us and we were able to see deep into each other's souls.

All of the images on my photo map are, in my mind, contained within that one house in Santa Fe. I imagine myself with loving relationships, intellectually challenged, making a contribution to others, in great health, creating an enduring legacy, spiritually aware, financially secure...all within that overarching lifestyle. I have but to glance at that house to remember what I'm working toward and why work, which used to occasionally seem mundane, is now always worth it.

Conclusion

The moment one definitely commits oneself,
then Providence moves too.

—Goethe

It's true, good things happen when you commit. You gain the benefit of the learning and experience curves—two very tangible advantages that are taught in every MBA program in the country, and the reason why companies like Dell Computer are almost impossible to imitate. There is also something almost magical about committing to a single direction, whether or not you choose to ring a big brass bell. Commitment helps you to become conscious of how mundane daily tasks are suddenly leading you toward vitally important lifetime goals.

Yet the world makes it difficult for the entrepreneur to commit. Resource poverty means that there are always ten tasks awaiting us. That in itself is a good excuse for not committing to any one of them. We dabble here and dabble there. The drive for growth at all costs means that we are always saying "yes" to our customers' demands, regardless of how this later impacts the soundness of our growth. The lack of available cash ensures that we can enjoy little time away from the business.

Committing to a narrow focus is an act of faith. That's what Goethe was talking about in the quote above. Determining to be the best in your niche, to carefully select customers, to lock them into you and optimize your pricing all require some nerve. But this philosophy is the only way that 99% of small business owners will succeed to the degree they once imagined. And, a "less is more" approach is the only way that you will make room in your life for what truly matters. I could never have foreseen being asked by The University of Texas Business School to join their faculty and teach courses in small business, even though this was something that beautifully supported my long-term goals. And, until I took the risk of committing to writing full time, I would never have accepted the position—I wouldn't have had the time if I had been working 50 hours a week in a "real job." One of the defining symbols of my lifetime goals to date—this book—would never have been written. Opportunities present themselves when you commit to the path that is true for you.

You can achieve everything that is important to you once you have accepted that you must do less before you can do more. However, it is not just business activities that we must consider giving up. Giving up certain personal and social activities can foster resentment in others and create a feeling of selfishness or guilt within ourselves. For example, if you give up playing on your company's softball team so that you can apply that six hours a week to painting, or practicing the piano or working on that new business plan, you are almost certain to be attacked by some for your "selfishness." What this means, of course, is that those who attack you have little concern for what matters most to *you*—they've probably never even asked.

Or, maybe you've always coached Little League. Oh yes, where our children and other family members are involved, cuts to our time budget are especially difficult, often fraught with resentment and guilt. So I'll offer my philosophy: The greatest gift you can give to those you love, whether nine or 90 years old, is your permission for *them* to pursue *their* own goals in life. And there is no other way to give this gift honestly than to lead by example. If you "sacrifice" who you are and what you are capable of for others, the only message you can possibly be sending them is that they must someday do the same. Is that really the message you meant to convey?

I use the word "permission" in this context because Nelson Mandela once used it in a powerful speech. Here is a man who understands commitment. His words are among the most inspiring that I have ever read. I often think of them before tough personal decisions that I know others may view as selfish.

> *Our deepest fears are not that we are inadequate. Our deepest fear is that we are powerful beyond measure. It is our light, not our darkness that most frightens us. We ask ourselves, who am I to be brilliant, gorgeous, talented and fabulous? Actually, who are you not to be? You are a child of God. Your playing small doesn't serve the world. There is nothing enlightening about shrinking so that other people won't feel insecure around you. We were born to make manifest the glory of God that is within us. It's not just in some of us; it's in everyone. As we let our own light shine, we unconsciously give other people permission to do the same. As we are liberated from our fear, our presence automatically liberates others.*

By making the tough choices to give up unproductive activities, and replace them with actions that honor what's most important in your life, you unconsciously give others permission to do the same. What greater gift could you possibly give to those you care about?

What is the most important word in business? Focus. What is the most important word in life? Focus. It is a clear, visible focus that will link the daily business activities that matter directly to your lifetime goals—your photo map. It is this focus, this commitment, that will determine whether your greatest asset—your time—is wasted, or used as supercharged fuel.

Only you can decide what to focus on, and that very decision will determine whether you achieve your goals and dreams. That's the power of the photo map—a simple but powerful reminder of what you are working towards. Don't play small; dream the Big Dream. Liberate someone. Start with yourself and start today. If you can survive, you can thrive—the difference is razor thin.

Your business or your life?

I hope by now the answer is clear; the answer is *both!*

Index